NECK DEEP
AND OTHER PREDICAMENTS

NECK DEEP

AND OTHER PREDICAMENTS

Ander Monson

Graywolf Press
SAINT PAUL, MINNESOTA

Publication of this volume is made possible in part by a grant provided by the Minnesota State Arts Board, through an appropriation by the Minnesota State Legislature; a grant from the Wells Fargo Foundation Minnesota; and a grant from the National Endowment for the Arts, which believes that a great nation deserves great art. Significant support has also been provided by the Bush Foundation; Target; the McKnight Foundation; and other generous contributions from foundations, corporations, and individuals. To these organizations and individuals we offer our heartfelt thanks.

The Graywolf Press Nonfiction Prize is funded in part by endowed gifts from the Arsham Ohanessian Charitable Remainder Unitrust and the Ruth Easton Trust of the Edelstein Family Foundation.

Published by Graywolf Press
2402 University Avenue, Suite 203
Saint Paul, Minnesota 55114
All rights reserved.

www.graywolfpress.org

Published in the United States of America
Printed in Canada

ISBN-13: 978-1-55597-459-6
ISBN-10: 1-55597-459-7

2 4 6 8 9 7 5 3 1
First Graywolf Printing, 2007

Library of Congress Control Number: 2006929500

Cover design: Kyle G. Hunter

Cover art: © Veer

ACKNOWLEDGMENTS

My gratitude to the editors of the following publications where the essays below first appeared:

American Nerd: The Long Crush

Bellingham Review: Index for X and the Origin of Fires

The Cincinnati Review: Cranbrook Schools: Adventures in Bourgeois Topologies

The Florida Review: Subject to Wave Action: A There and a Back (with Orchestral Accompaniment)

Ninth Letter: Failure: A Meditation, Another Iteration (with Interruptions)

A Public Space: Afterword: Elegy for Telegram and *Starflight*

Quarterly West: I Have Been Thinking about Snow

Seneca Review: Outline toward a Theory of the Mine Versus the Mind and the Harvard Outline; Fragments: On Dentistry

CONTENTS

Whether a book includes a dedication at all, to whom it is dedicated, and the phrasing of the dedication are matters for the author to determine. It may be suggested, however, that the word "Dedicated" is superfluous; a simple "To" is sufficient. It is not necessary to identify (or even to give the whole name of) the person to whom the work is dedicated, nor is it necessary to give the life dates of a person who has died; but both are permissible. Extravagant dedications are things of the past. A dedication intended to be humorous will very likely lose its humor with time and so is inappropriate in a serious book destined to take a permanent place in the literature.

—The Chicago Manual of Style, 13th Edition

Thus, to M.,
and you, and you, and you

JUDGE'S STATEMENT

Ander Monson is so cunning and quick-witted as an essayist that it's almost easy to miss just how touching, how human, how stubbornly elegiac his writing can be. To propose, for instance, that Monson is perhaps the most formally adventurous inquisitor of our new information technologies, risks—as James Merrill once observed in another context—"rubbing silver with quicksilver." The trendy glamour of a phrase like *formally adventurous inquisitor of our new information technologies* simultaneously enlivens and cheapens my praise, also ignoring as well the quirkiest, likely the boldest aspects of his stoic accomplishments.

Monson is as gaga about gadgets, diagrams, and recondite technical skills as any other modern gearhead. Yet he remains fascinated—and troubled—by all the incidental organizational forms around and inside our knowledge, old or new. Not only the Internet, but the index, the list, the telegram, the fragment, the quotation, the novel, the memoir, the vaunted scientific study, the lowly outline, and conspicuously the essay. "I have always loved methods of communication," he notes, "the idea of complicated networks, of impossibly complex systems." Monson celebrates such systems as "charms against aloneness" and "ways out of the labyrinth." But obsessive and playful, engrossed and deadpan, delighting over complex schemata but alert to their limits, and often most personal when most abstract, he writes out of a literary/scientific tradition that recalls the skeptical experiments of Pliny or Plutarch.

Hence, I think, Monson's elegiac strain, his pathos, his appreciation for the ghosts inside his machines, mechanical or verbal. "If there is form, then there must be failure of form," he remarks at the start of his brilliant, fractured investigation, "Failure: A Meditation, Another Iteration (with Interruptions)." By "failure" here Monson intends (among other notions) our many verbal and epistemological hauntings—our "thousands of dead literary magazines" as well as the latest "ghost web sites," our myriad "forms of Dead Media" past to present. "I know something about the constituency of failure geeks," he says, and in another essay, "Afterword: Elegy for Telegram and *Starflight*," goes on to prove it:

> Technology enthusiasts know all about self-consciousness and obsolescence. At one point I fancied myself one of them—the geeky, the necessarily obsolete. I love old computer systems, the Amiga, the Commodore 64, the Adam, the NeXT, the old Macintoshes that you can *mod* (modify) to work as fishbowls now or simply clocks. I love the old technology—the spindles of punch cards, corrugated boxes of eight-inch floppy disks (now floppy disks of any kind—and we usually mean the physically floppy 5¼" disks, not the stiffer 3½" so-called floppy disks, when we say *floppy*—are obsolete), 8-pin dot-matrix printers that would hum and perforate every character in every line. I still have a stack of eight-inch floppy disks. . . .

Failure geeks, indeed! Permit me to note here just how linked, even interchangeable are Monson's memorial and comic guises. Is this inventory of vanished technologies nostalgic or ludicrous, smart-ass or pitiable? But as he also writes, this time in his elegant rather than geeky mode, "I love the idea of failure in art—the failed experiment . . . the beautiful wreck, the stalled fragment."

Monson, as his title, *Neck Deep and Other Predicaments*, indicates, is a recidivist master of what he calls "immersion." Whether plunged into snow or water, whether his interior excavations occur in a dentist's chair or in the mines of his Michigan childhood, and whether he is brooding on a boat or on a bench in the courtyard of a fancy school that once expelled him, Monson works from so far inside his subjects that his ingenious verbal structures can seem only the skeletal configurations of sawdust and debris left after the departed insects. "And there is the pleasure of obsession itself," he asserts in "The Long Crush," his slacker-overdrive paean to disc golf, "immersion in the world of esoteric detail even in spite of (or maybe because of) the derision of *patzers* who just don't get it, what it is to lose yourself so completely in something, and who cares, finally, what?" This immersion is often in a language—the vernaculars of mining, for instance, or snow—and sometimes in a language of intellectual and emotional bewilderment. "I Have Been

Thinking about Snow" cites the *OED* definition of "flurry"—"To bewilder or confuse as by haste or noise; to agitate, 'put out'"—and there Monson recalls playing with his brother:

> I used to demand that my brother cover me over with snow until it weighed so much that I could not move. My head would pop out of the patted-down bank like a Whack-a-Mole. My brother would begin to pelt me with snowballs. That weight would feel so good above me. Watch my body lose its heat. Watch this body lose its heat to the weight of nature packed hard above me. He'd pretend to run away and leave me there. When I got cold enough that I could no longer tell the difference between outside and in, I'd blink my eyes three times, which meant unbury me, let me back up into your world.

The intricate shapes of Monson's essays, the devastating Harvard outline, particularly, or what might appear as only spasms down the page of random words and dots, are what every reader will notice first about *Neck Deep and Other Predicaments*. Collectively these fluid, divergent shapes direct a dismantling and reinvention of the essay as an instrument for thought, an option for writing, and represent further immersion, still another pleasurable, dangerous confusion of the "difference between outside and in." Monson's essays blur scaffolding and building, topic and design. "Admittedly, everything is complicated," as he writes in the meditation on snow, "is beautiful and intricate, infinitely recursive, when seen closely." But few essayists have so insistently engaged— and then embodied—that complication and beauty. His work joins a literary/scientific mode that he tags "topology," sometimes defined as the science of place, but more specifically glossed by Monson as, "about electricity or water or anything that flows equally throughout a form, that moves through channels." As he elaborates in "Cranbrook Schools: Adventures in Bourgeois Topologies"—elaborates and *personalizes*: "Today I am looking for connections—both my own to the place and to my questionable past, and between myself and the body of knowledge that informs the design of the place; I am looking for connectivity and resistance to transformation. . . . I am trying hard to think about this place, and my place in it, in topological terms."

Fascinatingly, "Cranbrook Schools" focuses on a moment not of sexual but of aesthetic awakening and coming-of-age. Monson's essays are set at the intersection of place and self. "This place has made me, is in turn made for me," he calculates. "This is turning into a theorem: Cranbrook offers a designed aesthetic experience in order to produce a certain kind of student, person, aesthete, citizen."

The "Harvard Outline" essay concentrates the alloyed grandeur of aesthetic shapes:

> iv. how there's a pressure from the outside structure
>   1. how the structure
>   a. either binds you in or wants to expel you like a sickness
>   b. think the mine, the outline, as a body
>   c. an ecosystem
>   d. or a mechanical spring
>   i. compress
>   ii. release
>   iii. repeat
> v. and that structure creates pressure; how architecture is the elegant distribution of stress

Monson never elides the autobiographical underpinnings, and the implicit hazards (fear, swagger, even "wankery") of his own exhaustive structures:

> 1. the ethics and economics of the writing act
>   a. and that other pressure it entails
>   i. so maybe the outline is a kind of architecture I am trying to erect
>   ii. to protect myself against my family, meaninglessness, and the future
>   1. an artifice to get inside the past
>   2. like a cold and unlit hole—what family tragedy is there behind me glittering like a vein
>   iii. perhaps it is a womb

1. and this then has to do with my
mother's death
2. a protective sheath, a comfort zone
iv. or it could be a shell
b. an attempt for rigor as some buffer or protection
c. or maybe it is elegance for the sake of it
d. an infinite recursion
e. some wankery

Granted, then, that at once frustrating, gorgeous, and hilarious, Monson's essays look the way they do at least in part because his world looks the way it does, what else might such designs get him? One vantage is speed—I can think of few essays that move as fast, or will as promptly and dexterously open up large political and cultural vistas from local, nearly private fixations. Another vantage, surprisingly, is candor. For the Monson of *Neck Deep and Other Predicaments* introspection and intricacy, elaboration and intimacy, all are bound together, and I'd argue that his formal schemes lead him into direct, even naked statements that might otherwise sound sentimental, familiar, unearned. "Outline toward a Theory of the Mine Versus the Mind and the Harvard Outline" and "I Have Been Thinking about Snow" fall among the toughest and most moving accounts of fathers and sons in contemporary writing.

Monson is also a poet (*Vacationland*), a novelist (*Other Electricities*), and an editor (the online magazine *DIAGRAM*), as well as an essayist. But how circumstantial, how contingent, how spongy, these disciplines and classifications can seem when you encounter the mix of fact, poetry, fiction, and collage in this book you—I'm almost sure it's you—hold in your hands.

"The other excellence about the bath is the plunge into it," Monson insists, "the pleasures of the first immersion. I use this language when I think how good literature acts on me (literature as a force that acts on the body)." And so now it's time to take that plunge, turn the page, experience that pleasure of first immersion.

—Robert Polito
New Paltz, New York
July 2006

NECK DEEP

AND OTHER PREDICAMENTS

OUTLINE TOWARD A THEORY OF THE MINE VERSUS THE MIND AND THE HARVARD OUTLINE

I. Start with the Roman numeral I with an authoritative period trailing just after it. This is the Harvard Outline, which comes in Caps and is a method of organizing information
   a. remembered from high school as a major step toward creating an essay
       i. though there was a decimal method, too
   b. but I've never been comfortable with the thing—its seeming rigor, its scaffolding so white against the language
       i. never felt the top-down structuralist method of constructing writing to be useful or effective; the mind, so idiosyncratic, unusual
           1. its strangeness and its often-incoherence
               a. the lovely anomaly
   c. and the Harvard Outline is the reason that I get 55 5-paragraph essays every month
   d. it is, I think, suspect, (its
   e. headings
       i. subheadings
           1. sub-subheadings
               a. etc.
               b. though there is a pleasure to this iteration, this recursion—like mathematics and the algorithms I played with and admired in computer-science classes, writing functions that called themselves
                   i. which called themselves
                       1. which called themselves
                           a. until they were satisfied

        2. and exited

      ii. right back

  c. out

      i. like those Russian nesting [Matryoshka] dolls; a lovely symmetry; such satisfaction comes in nesting

      ii. such starkness

        1. elegance)

f. all those steps out and down across the page—like the writing task is that of going downhill, like a waterfall in its rush

    i. or the incremental, slow plod down the slope, skis buried behind in some drift

g. While technically called "The Harvard Outline"

    i. it has nothing to do with Harvard

      1. according to their archivists, "it appears to be a generic term"

    ii. so it's difficult to track it down in the history of organizing information

      1. which is what this culture spends increasing time (and money!) doing

        a. witness the amazing success of the search engine Google

          i. as created by Larry Page and Sergey Brin

          ii. with its elegant mechanism of concordance

            1. of ranking searches by the number of pages that link to each individual page or site in order to establish the relative importance of that initial page or site

              a. and look—there's no need for parentheses in 1. above thanks to the Harvard Outline

              b. again that attraction to self-examination

        c. again that attraction to
           what elegance there is to
           find

II. My family has a background in the Michigan mining industry
  a. a history in copper, iron, the cast-off leftover materials necessary to process ore from rock
  b. though less my recent family
     i. not my father who is a professor—whose job, like mine, is (reductively) the mining and refining, then the distribution of information for (small sums of) money
       1. though perhaps this is a cynical view of the profession
         a. and light-as-knowledge metaphor is hardly breaking new ground
       2. still I like the image of the light-helmeted professor plowing through the darkness
         a. though it is romantic to say the least
       3. "like mine" (from above)—mining is a story of possession
         a. of legal ownership of land and rights, the permission to go below the crust
       4. "breaking new ground" (from above)—again the construction terminology
         a. the invocation of the building, of the engineering
       5. my father teaches at Michigan Technological University, formerly the Michigan College of Mines, a school that is just about to lose its Mining Engineering program
         a. which is older than the oldest living humans
         b. which is "one of only 15 mining engineering programs in the U.S. that has been uninterrupted since the beginning of the century and has also held accreditation with the Accreditation Board for Engineering and Technology (ABET)

since 1936" according to the MTU
Mining Engineering web site

    i. this tidbit brought to you by Google

    ii. this tidbit being no longer accurate
(now we should use past tense, as
the program has been retired, killed,
phased out): this is an information
shift between the writing of the essay
and its publication

c. but further back

    i. since nearly everyone who emigrated to Upper Michigan
from (mostly) Scandinavia worked in the mines, or
worked in industries that supported it

        1. the mining boom in the 19th century was so big
that Calumet, Michigan, population of 879 as of
the 2000 census, was nearly named the capital of
Michigan

        2. and there are stories of exploitation and immense
hardship

            a. as there always are

        3. though just after WWII, the price of copper de-
clined and so—though there's still plenty underneath the northern earth—the mines slowly shut
their doors

            a. now there are no active producing mines left
in the Keweenaw

                i. the railroads no longer run

                ii. even the Greyhound bus service has
stopped

                iii. it felt at times while growing up like
living in a dead-letter office

                    1. another information shift: evi-
dently there are still two mines
that remain in operation, one of
my which my high school friend
Jeremy, his father a metallurgist,
is working for

      b. though the shells they left behind—the fine network of tunnels that still riddle the earth—are havens for millions of bats

          i. who come out at night through the chicken wire that often covers up the mines' mouths

          ii. and were—until recently, when the method of closing off the mines was changed to be a bit more bat-friendly—picked off by hundreds of raccoons that would sit at the chicken wire, waiting for the daily exodus and feast

      c. and now Upper Michigan is a destination for bat-watching tourists

d. and anyone growing up in the Keweenaw has had ready access to mines

      i. either through the tours of the few remaining open tourist mines

          1. which are absolutely worth doing, though expensive (to the tune of $25), because to be submerged a mile underneath the earth is a necessary experience

              a. to get that absolute darkness

                  i. even if you think you know what it's like

              b. and to get that absolute *chill*

              c. to know what your ancestors went through

                  i. or at least to have an idea—isn't this an honor or an obligation?

      ii. or more likely illegally

          1. breaking the locks off the doors

              a. because there are hundreds of old shafts sunk in the land that haven't been filled

          2. drinking inside (also arguably a family obligation), or exploring with rope, flashlights, and a constant sense of possibility

              a. for there is something beautiful, nearly un-bearable, about a hole in the earth

        i. about darkness
            1. that unknown
                a. black box
                    i. big X
                ii. maybe it's a male fixation
            b. that it must bear exploration, no matter how far down it goes
                i. maybe it's too many Hardy Boys books, or Jules Verne
            c. and also there's the danger
                i. a definite attraction
                    1. one cure for boredom
                    2. a cheapie and dangerous carnival ride
   iii. or possibly through the few research mines maintained by the University
            1. one of which I discovered while hiking in Hancock, Michigan
                a. while it's not a public mine, it is not gated or barred off
                b. walk within a quarter of a mile and you'll feel the drop in temperature caused by the cool air streaming out
                    i. a counterintuitive finding—remember high school geology, the earth's crust, mantle, core, etc., and lava bursting out through craters
                  ii. or Jules Verne again
                      1. while less than absolutely reliable
               iii. and how it gets hotter now
                    1. the further
                        a. in
                          i. you go
               iv. how there's a pressure from the outside structure
                    1. how the structure

        a. either binds you in or wants to expel you like a sickness

        b. think the mine, the outline, as a body

        c. an ecosystem

        d. or a mechanical spring

            i. compress

            ii. release

            iii. repeat

     v. and that structure creates pressure; how architecture is the elegant distribution of stress

III. The outline, so like a mine

    a. defined by penetration

       i. deeper in

      ii. both laterally and vertically

         1. for harder information

      iii. yes, how male, again, you dirty bird

    b. and mining is interested mostly in the horizontal

       i. mineral deposits—in the absence of fault or other geologic strangeness—lay naturally in planes

      ii. since similar materials respond similarly to pressure, they settle horizontally

      iii. and the goal of the miner is to identify the deposit

         1. in terms of *dip and strike*

            a. the straight line of maximum inclination (*dip*)

            b. the horizontal line, the contour line (*strike*)

    c. and the vertical when necessary, to either follow the vein

       i. or to proceed deeper into the earth once the vein has been exhausted

    d. though the terminology of the mine is far more lovely than of the outline

       i. *level, incline, drifts, shaft, crosscut, winze, raise* and *mouth* and *face, gossan, apex, shaft, adit, gangue, stope*

ii. *"Shallow Boring in Soft Rocks: Boring by Hand Auger"*
  1. chapter subheading from the "Boring" chapter,
     Introduction to Mining by Bohuslav Stoces
iii. having an essential mystery to them
  1. due to their inaccessibility
      a. compare to that of the Harvard Outline,
         designed particularly (one imagines—though
         it's not clear who designed it) to be easily
         negotiable
  2. and the aura of danger, of esoteric, academic, secret
     knowledge about them
      a. they literally describe loci of danger, pits and
         sinkholes; they offer both treasure and death
          i. both of which have a lure
iv. and I was obsessed with mining for the first 10 years of my
    life
  1. visiting the A. E. Seaman Mineralogical Museum at
     Michigan Technological University
      a. which has the 17-ton copper boulder, the
         largest mineral specimen ever taken from
         Lake Superior
      b. an emblem of the Keweenaw, one of the
         world's richest copper deposits
  2. trying to convince my dad to buy me various geo-
     logical supplies
      a. such as the rock tumbler I never really
         used—a sad emblem of my childhood sitting
         on a shelf maybe in my parents' basement
  3. agate hunting along the shores of Lake Superior
  4. looking for chunks of unrefined copper in the
     woods or in the hills of stampsand along Portage
     Canal (the canal that cuts off the tip of the
     Keweenaw Peninsula from Michigan)
      a. leftovers from processing iron ore
      b. which very well may be poisoning some
         Michigan lakes

        i. and we try not to think too much about this

     5. making homemade explosives according to the often-poor instructions from Paladin Press books and other, even less reliable sources

        a. ceasing only when a good friend of mine lost 3 fingers

  v. and in a way, I still am—as it's the central story of the place where I am from, the big goodness and the tragedy

     1. it is how I imagine the ghost of slavery is to Southern writers

        a. having this central, public history contributes to there even being such a thing as a "Southern Writer," whereas there aren't as obviously "Northern Writers"

     2. (the boom and the bust—the makings of story itself)

        a. and certainly the makings of much of my family

e. perhaps it's only my desire

  i. that this, my kind of work

     1. darkness on light onscreen, then on the page

  ii. be worth as much as what my family did in the dark for hours, for days, for years

f. and the metaphor of mining one's past or childhood for writing material

  i. an apt construction, experience as *material*

  ii. is used a lot, and is something I'm concerned about myself

     1. the ethics and the economics of the writing act

        a. and that other pressure it entails

           i. so maybe the outline is a kind of architecture I am trying to erect

          ii. to protect myself against my family, meaninglessness, and the future

             1. an artifice to get inside the past

    2. like a cold and unlit hole—what
      family tragedy is there behind
      me glittering like a vein
   iii. perhaps it is a womb
     1. and this then has to do with my
       mother's death
     2. a protective sheath, a comfort
       zone
   iv. or it could be a shell
  b. an attempt for rigor as some buffer or protec-
    tion
  c. or maybe it is elegance for the sake of it
  d. an infinite recursion
  e. some wankery
 2. then there's always the possibility of being stuck,
  candle snuffed by a sudden blast
  a. the candles that my family would have to buy
    themselves and carry—lit—down into the
    earth, the candles that were the only protec-
    tion against the emptiness and isolation
 3. with no way of lighting up again, and no way
ii. back out—

I HAVE BEEN THINKING ABOUT SNOW.......

.... and the way to get inside it, like through the entrance of an ice maze during Winter Carnival, Michigan Technological University's yearly festival of snow, where the Greeks and other student organizations build ice sculptures sometimes fifty feet deep and high out of carefully packed snow.....................

.... This was one of my pleasures as a child—winding through the tunnels they would carve, carving our own in the snowbanks that would sometimes rise above ten feet high around the yard...........................

.... Partially this is because I have gone so long without it, living in Alabama........................

.... People in Alabama are mystified and terrified by it. The forecasts are big news if they can predict even the possibility, the one-in-twenty chance of it gathering around dust particles in the clouds and descending indirectly to the earth. James Spann, meteorologist on ABC 33/40, a Birmingham station, is very excited to predict that we might receive some precipitation. This is a great moment for him. You can see it in the lines around his mouth as they crease and bend. There are lines around the block at the liquor store. Runs on canned goods and milk at Bruno's, the local "gourmet" grocery-store chain, which is run by the same company as the less-uppity and apparently duller Food World. We have not received much yet this winter, but there is talk. . . . .

. . . . The University of Alabama cancelled classes two years ago on just the threat of snow. All my students trudged home, fearing and expectant. Although none came. . . . . .

. . . .

. . . . When I was in New York over Christmas 2002, there were only rinds around the curbs. I thought about peeling some away and bringing them home to Alabama in a Zip-loc bag. There is the problem of melting, however. Would the snow be the same when I came home. Would I have to keep it on ice or frozen in order to keep it snow? Or could I let it melt then freeze it once home. Would it then be snow, or would it just be dirty New York ice. . . . .

. . . .

. . . . I asked my father to send some snow from my home in Houghton, Michigan, about as far north as you can go in Michigan's Upper Peninsula. We get 250+ inches a year there. I thought he could send me some on ice in Ziploc bags, freeze-packed and FedExed. . . . . . .

. . . .

. . . . They haven't had much yet this year. Every e-mail I get from him contains an update on how much is on the ground, how much they are expecting, how many inches fell but melted, how many feet have accumulated, how much he cleared with one of his three snowblowers, which are all now in the shop. Which leaves him to clear it out by hand. Which used to be my job and my brother's job. Which we did not enjoy, but which we did of course. That's what the sons do in the winter. . . . .

. . . .

. . . . My grandmother—approaching ninety—refuses to let my father clear her walkway. . . . .

. . . .

. . . .

. . . .

. . . . . She is not technically my grandmother, but my step-grandmother. If that makes sense. She usually clears her own snow but sometimes she cannot, and so my father does it secretly. Sometimes when she realizes this she gets angry, but it is a risk that he likes to take. . . . .

. . . .

. . . .

. . . . *1829* Virginia Lit. Museum *16 Dec. 418 Blizzard, a violent blow.* [OED] . . . .

. . . .

. . . . *1881* N.Y. Nation *184 The hard weather has called into use a word which promises to become a national Americanism, namely 'blizzard'. It designates a storm (of snow and wind) which men cannot resist away from shelter.* [OED] . . . .

. . . .

. . . .

. . . .

. . . . Think blizzard, think flurry in terms of boxing. A rain of blows. Many meteorological terms make that particular transition. Think fist as force. Think the body as a matter of nature. . . . .

. . . .

. . . . I saw flakes today. Some minor evidence of potential weather. You do see frost starring everything on the ground.

. . . .

. . . . Of course the weather matters to the growers a great deal, whether Midwestern or Southern. One reason why everyone in Michigan talks about it all the time. . . . .

. . . .

. . . . Frost—even a dip in the temperature—can be catastrophic to the orange-growing industry, especially in Florida. Where they admittedly do not get much snow. . . . .

. . . .

. . . . Where my brother lives for the time being. He does not miss the snow. . . . .

. . . .

. . . .

. . . . How can you not miss the snow, when you've lived most of your life in the half-year winters of Upper (far north of the area that residents call "Northern") Michigan? . . . .

. . . .

. . . . *"The upper level pattern over North America is domi-nated by a huge vortex over eastern Canada and a large ridge just off the Pacific Coast. The jet stream splits around the Pacific ridge, with the sub-tropical jet racing across the southern half of the country. The subtropical flow is bringing a good bit of moisture in at high levels, resulting in a beau-tiful pattern of high clouds across Alabama."* — ABC 33/40, Birmingham, Alabama, 02/09/03. . . . .

. . . .

. . . .

. . . .

. . . .

. . . . It is very difficult for professional meteorologists to predict the weather with any accuracy more than four or five days in advance. . . . . .

. . . .

. . . .

Although how hard could it be, I think. . . . .

. . . .

. . . . Admittedly, everything is complicated, is beautiful and intri-cate, infinitely recursive, when seen closely. . . . .

. . . .

. . . .

. . . .

. . . .

. . . . A string of tornadoes came through Tuscaloosa and western Alabama in November 2001 and November 2002, doing huge amounts of damage. They decimated a just-about-to-open grocery store next to a local community college entirely, but did not touch the college buildings. The tornado system in 2001 was followed by weeks of freezing temperatures, with over 30,000 Alabama residents without power for days. . . . .

. . . .

. . . .

. . . . *Which men cannot resist away from shelter.* . . . .
. . . .
. . . .
. . . .
. . . . Culture is the opposite of weather. Is a hedge against it. Is a
fight beneath it. Is a losing fight a boxing match a match struck in hard
wind and extinguished immediately. . . . .
. . . .
. . . .
. . . . Consider the threat of mass ex-
tinction at the hands of one of the trillion comets or midsize and up as-
teroids that we will not see until they hurtle right into us, raise a hundred
square kilometers of the ocean, fog us over, kill us off. . . . .
. . . .
. . . .
. . . .
. . . . Is snow a lack or a mass. The white
suggests the lack, but such weight! I used to demand that my brother
cover me over with snow until it weighed so much that I could not move.
My head would pop out of the patted-down bank like a Whack-a-Mole.
My brother would begin to pelt me with snowballs. That weight would
feel so good above me. Watch my body lose its heat. Watch this body lose
its heat to the weight of nature packed hard above me. He'd pretend to
run away and leave me there. When I got cold enough that I could no
longer tell the difference between outside and in, I'd blink my eyes three
times, which meant unbury me, let me back up into your world. . . . .
. . . .
. . . . The body's amazing temperature
control keeps the temp. right around 98.6. Mine was closer to 99.1 most
days. The doctors always told me that it was normal. I am sure it is.
How come my brother's was always low—98.3 or so. If the body can't
tolerate much of a dip in temperature—like orange trees in Florida—why
is there a difference from one body to another. . . . .
. . . .
. . . . I have been thinking
about snow, or its lack. Would I really want to live away from it for long.
Away from the reasonable possibility of it. Away from the expectation

of its mounting force. Away from all that white along the eyes. Away from sunburn on bright days when the sun reflects off the gleaming snow—the only way of course we can see the gleaming snow is the sun—and on the skin. And who thinks to wear sunscreen in middle January?

. . . .
. . . .
. . . .
. . . . Artificial snow machines. Generating the necessary inches for the lodges at Ski Brule to operate, to keep the tourists coming in, to keep the ski lifts running and the tourists coming down the mountain, moving side to side, leaving their horde of zigzag slalom tracks. . . . .
. . . .
. . . .
. . . . Artificial snow is real snow. It is made in the same way that true snow is. Except that it's gunned from nozzles at 350 to 400 psi, breaking the water into very tiny particles that are easier to freeze. Highly compressed air is gunned from nozzles into the atomized water, which causes the water to freeze as the air expands. A fan sucks the new snow out and fires it on the slopes and on the tracks. . . . .
. . . .
. . . .
. . . .
. . . . There's no such thing as cold . . . . .
. . . . in physics . . . .
. . . . just the lack of heat, of molecular motion. . . . .
. . . .
. . . . It takes a lot of water to make snow. It takes a lot of electricity to make snow. . . . .
. . . .
. . . .
. . . .
. . . . 53,712,000 pounds of water per day equals 1 foot of snow on a 2-lane road that is 10 miles long. . . . .
. . . .
. . . .
. . . .

. . . . Artificial snow was first introduced and used for skiing on Mt. Greylock in Massachusetts. Artificial snow was invented in 1946. . .

. . . . And why an artificial snow? . . . .

. . . . Aside from the economic necessity for ski runs and slopes, to extend the skiing season, to compensate for the whim of nature whose patterns we cannot yet predict far out with any accuracy. . . . .

. . . . A flurry is—one definition—*the death-throes of a dying whale* [OED] . . . .

. . . . so think Melville, think obsession, think big and white and gone . . .

. . . . and I am gone, and I am thinking about never coming back to the snow country for any appreciable length of time. . . . .

. . . .
. . . .
. . . . I am thinking about snow and structure. . . . . . .
. . . Is there an order to it / pattern in it / evidence of God or atom force. . .
. . . . . William A. Bentley photographed snowflakes on slides for years. .
. . . . He found regularities, symmetries. . . . .
. . . . The photographs are stunning, lovely. . . . .
. . . .
. . . . Some claimed he'd faked them . . . .
. . . . found an order . . . .
. . . .
. . . . where there logically was none . . . .
. . . . that they were *too perfect* and couldn't exist in nature. . . . .
. . . .
. . . .
. . . .
. . . .
. . . . I am thinking of the tracks my boots make in the snow.
Irrevocable except by act of God or weather or a movement of the heart.
Or intentional disruption with a pine branch. Still there would be a mark.
. . . .
. . . .
. . . . some indication of obfuscation. . . . .
. . . .
. . . .
. . . . The snow they
had in New York barely qualified. It was the last gasp of a storm left for
days on the streets. Getting black and dirty. If I brought it home, it would
melt into water, sand, and cigarette ash. Refreeze it to turn it to an awful
Popsicle. . . . .
. . . .
. . . .
. . . . Several years ago in my hometown
in Michigan, two men robbed a bank in the heart of January on a snowmobile. The police followed the tracks back to their cabin and arrested
them. They only had $22,000. It's hard to carry much more in bills,
though the movies would like you to believe otherwise. . . . .

. . . .

. . . .

. . . . I am thinking of snow and crime, of snow and drunkenness. Number of churches. Number of bars. Number of county jails. The ratio between. . . . .

. . . .

. . . .

. . . .

. . . . . Number of times I have gone through the ice in my dreams. . . . . . .

. . . .

. . . . Number of snowmobiles sold as opposed to cars in the northern half of Michigan. . .

. . . .

. . . .

. . . . Number of tickets given to snowmobiles. . . . .

. . . . Most snowmobiles can go 60 miles an hour on open, well-packed snow. . . . .

. . . .

. . . .

. . . .

. . . . A fast-moving snowmobile can move over open water for miles. . .

. . . .

. . . . and they even have summer water snowmobile races. . . . .

. . . .

. . . . a kid I knew from high school, not someone I particularly liked . . .

. . . . (in fact I disliked him inasmuch as one can in high school . . .

. . . . given one's own predilection for asininity). . . . .

. . . . is now a semiprofessional racer . . . .

. . . . of both snowmobiles and Jet Skis . . . .

. . . .

. . . . —what does this mean, I ask myself— . . . .

. . . .

. . . .

. . . . Number of dollars brought in by snowmobile tourism . . . .

. . . . Number of deaths brought in by snowmobile tourism . . . .

. . . .

. . . .

. . . . *1883* Let. *in* Advance *1 Mar., Driving snow, with very blizzardly tendencies. 1888* San Francisco News Let. *(Farmer), I should like to have seen the Colonel's face when he got that very cold blizzardy letter. 1892 GUNTER Miss Dividends I. vi. 67 Then he suddenly ejaculates 'Well I'm blizzarded!' 1946* Chicago Daily News *5 Mar. 8/4 [It] would ruin the disposition of the throngs...especially on blizzardy nights* [OED]. . . . .

. . . .

. . . .

. . . .

. . . .

. . . .

. . . .

. . . . fig. *1820 J. Q. ADAMS* Mem. *2 June (1875) V. 137 His flurries of temper pass off as quickly as they rise* [OED] . . . .

. . . .

. . . .

. . . . the storm as a function of temper. . . . .

. . . . . . the temper of the weatherman or my father. . . . .

. . . .

. . . . . When my father used to drink, we would be afraid of his temper. .

. . . .

. . . .

. . . . (not afraid of physical violence exactly . . . .

. . . . and this is no different than fear of any father . . . .

. . . . but of something else, maybe of his shadow . . . .

. . . . of isolation, disapproval, one of many sorts of weather patterns) . . .

. . . .

. . . .

. . . .

. . . . and even seven states away I find that I still am, much to my wife's annoyance . . . .

. . . .

. . . . although it (my fear and my wife's annoyance) . . . .

. . . . . . is mostly Midwestern, contained, implicit—. . . . .

. . . .

. . . . like nukes on television, all duck and cover, all threat . . . .

. . . . and imminence, all interiority, potential energy on the edge . . .

. . . . . . of translation into kinetic—. . . . .
. . . .
. . . . We are all afraid in one way or another . . . .
. . . . of our parents and their judgments . . . .
. . . . of their wrath, interest in us, or lack thereof. . . .
. . . .
. . . .
. . . . . And now we are separated by a time zone, over a thousand miles,
a couple hundred page breaks, a political party, a generation, and the
threat of weather or its end. . . . .
. . . .
. . . . When my wife and I drive up
north for winter (she is from Minnesota, where they know cold), we
rarely make it to my home in Michigan without being blizzarded in and
staying nights in inexpensive hotels in places like Louisville, Kentucky,
where they can't handle snow, but where they get it often enough to be
a problem. . . . .
. . . .
. . . . Even crossing the
state line from Wisconsin into Upper Michigan, the snow is immediately a foot higher, the roads not so well graded, the public radio more
lonely and depressing, the nights a power of 10 darker . . . .
. . . .
. . . whether this is through some obscure intent or sheer weird chance. . .
. . . .
. . . .
. . . . In a blizzard, we pulled over to
the side of the road and listened to the story of the whale ship *Essex* and
its travails, on which *Moby-Dick* was based. . . . .
. . . .
. . . . Gruesome
stuff to say the least. . . . .
. . . .
. . . . this weather, this text, this consciousness, this spacing
out across the page . . . .
. . . .
. . . .

. . . .
. . . .
. . . .
. . . .
. . . .
. . . .
. . . . Such . . . .
. . . .
. . . .
. . . .
. . . .
. . . .
. . . .
. . . .
. . . .
. . . .
. . . .
. . . .
. . . .
. . . .
. . . .
. . . .
. . . .
. . . .
. . . .
. . . .
. . . .
. . . .
. . . .
. . . .
. . . .
. . . .
. . . .
. . . .
. . . .
. . . .

. . . . isolation . . . .

. . . .
. . . .
. . . . . . Such . . . .
. . . .
. . . .
. . . . staggering weight—that can collapse a
barn, hundreds of roofs yearly, particularly those with an insufficient
grade: someone has to push off all the snow, and that someone is the
father unless the father designates it to the sons. . . . .
. . . .
. . . . More weight than all the miles of atmosphere above us. . . . .
. . . .
. . . . More than all the minor matters of the heart that seem so large
and gauzy. . . . .
. . . .
. . . . But it's a good weight, one I have grown to love. . . . . . .
. . . .
. . . .
. . . .
. . . . So we are not just separated by distance but by act of God
or threat of act of God . . . .
. . . .
. . . . or by the threat of God himself. . . . .
. . . .
. . . . Is this by choice or is it accident. . . . .
. . . .
. . . .
. . . . There are a lot of accidents. . . . . . .
. . . .
. . . .
. . . .
. . . . *b. Chiefly U.S. A sharp and sudden shower; a sudden rush
(of birds)* [OED] . . . .
. . . .
. . . .
. . . .
. . . .

. . . . *Which men cannot resist away from shelter.* . . . .

. . . .

. . . .

. . . .

. . . . *1698 FRYER* Acc. E. India & P. *128* marg.,
Flurries from the Hills carry Men and Oxen down the Precipice. 1726-7
SWIFT Gulliver *I. i. 22 The boat was overset by a sudden flurry from the*
north. 1831 SCOTT Jrnl. 18 Nov., Wind..dies away in the morning, and
blows in flurries rather contrary. 1890 Pall Mall G. *3 Dec. 1/3 You may*
watch 'catspaws' and 'flurries' on their rapid way. [OED]. . . . .

. . . .

. . . .

. . . .

. . . . How rapidly do relationships decline? . . . .

. . . .

. . . .

. . . .

. . . . How much space does it
take around you to drive you to the bar when you've told yourself . . . . .

. . . .

. . . . over . . . .

. . . .

. . and over . . . .

. . . . that you wouldn't go again under any circumstances. . . . .

. . . .

. . . . Churches are perhaps first a house, the house of God,
a roof, a sanctuary, apex, narthex, model homes for the improvement of
our souls, arms stretched out above us, shelter, a form of shelter. . . . . . .

. . . .

. . . .

. . . . . . My parents stopped taking me to church when I stole the merit
badges from the Boy Scout trove kept in a closet by the kitchen. . . . .

. . . .

. . . . I felt that I deserved them for so many winters, so much weight borne under snow, so many skills demonstrated:
fire-building, vandalism, plagiarism, compromise-brokering, dodging
bottles and bottle rockets, anger management, living through the oblong

story of depression, weather, and wilderness survival. . . . .

. . . .

. . . .

. . . . *Flurry, 1.* trans. *To bewilder or confuse as by haste or noise; to agitate, 'put out.'* [OED]. . . . .

. . . .

. . . .

. . . .

. . . .

. . . . I have been thinking about snowdrifts and the feeling of falling in them again, losing whatever heat keeps the meat of the body alive and twitching. . . . . . .

. . . .

. . . .

. . . .

. . . I have been thinking about loss. . . . .

. . . . How each winter is the story of a burial . . . .

. . . . gradual . . . .

. . . .

. . . . (and each spring another revelation) .

. . . .

. . . .

. . . . a compilation . . . .

. . . . a complication . . . .

. . . . until we are up to our necks . .

. . . .

. . . .

. . . . in North . . . .

. . . . in enough . . . .

. . . .

. . . . in what we feel . . . .

. . . . what we contain . . . .

. . . . in what we are contained . . . .

. . . . in what we barely understand. . . . .

. . . .

. . . .

. . . .

CRANBROOK SCHOOLS:
ADVENTURES IN BOURGEOIS TOPOLOGIES

Although I am not proud of it, I am waiting here for a revelation. I am waiting for meaning, for my experience to unpack itself, for my criminal history to find a kind of home, some explanation, or maybe truce.

One among many, this courtyard (gorgeous, designed by the architect Eliel Saarinen along with the surrounding buildings and deserving of all the praise from international architectural and design circles) I once thought normal, everyday, a usual sort of beauty and stateliness, simply the place I went to school. I am sitting in one of the courtyards that make up the boys' school in Cranbrook-Kingswood, an elite private school in Bloomfield Hills, Michigan, the third richest city per capita in the country. About twenty minutes south of us is the wonderful wreck of Detroit in all its burned, evacuated glory.

Two Kingswood School girls walk by me as I sit. One has surprisingly large breasts (a fact that I am ashamed to notice and admit to you—and yet I do in the interests of full disclosure), and both are wearing short skirts, though it's only fifty degrees outside—this is a strange throwback day in southeastern Michigan, May 3rd, meaning cold temperatures, mild sun with memories and intermittent hail. These are the kind of girls for whom, when I was in high school here, I would have been all aflame, and yet amazed at their inaccessibility. These are the girls who have somehow imprinted themselves on me in the hormone daze of my teenage years.

I am the only one outside aside for the occasional student slipping between or cutting classes: the grounds are exceptionally quiet. I feel as if any moment I will be discovered and interrogated; I feel that I am intruding, that I have no right to this. I had to pass through a security gate on the way in—a necessary measure to protect the rich (tuition in 2003 was more than $29,000) and riches here—and I wonder if I am still on some no-fly list at the school, though that's of course unlikely now, and they didn't actually ask for my name at the gate, so barring some kind of super-homeland-security technology, I am completely incognito. I am disappointed at being just let right back in and surprised by my disappointment.

Truth: I will say that I was expelled from this beautiful and isolated place my senior year, though in actuality I was allowed to withdraw (under threat of outright expulsion—not exactly a concession). I have been kicked off campus twice since then, in the two years since I left. I think my name was on a list at the gate then, though there are other ways into the grounds, especially during the day. But it has been ten years, and this place no longer remembers me. My name is not carved into the brick and concrete pillars supporting the walkway that spans the courtyard I am in (this is not a metaphor—others are). My name is not here anywhere.

Dare: this return is daring, I tell myself. I am coming back to try to face up to and recover something from my past from this place that holds so much of it. Maybe I'm officially trespassing, an offense I can add to the litany of crimes I am party to, responsible for. I sort of hope I am a threat to something, but I can't say what.

A sculpture depicts two boys wrestling naked—an example of the classical physical experience Cranbrook would like to believe that it encourages: healthy bodies striving upward to knowledge and citizenship. In reality, it looks as though one kid is getting his ass kicked. Neither the place or the students kicked my ass. I enjoyed my years here. I belonged—and that's something, to feel like you belong at all, especially in high school—to the group of boarding students, the reigning underclass (compare the one-third of students who board, typically attending on scholarship, to the other two-thirds: day students, who are almost to the man rich as shit, sons and daughters of Iacoccas, Penskes, Fords, etc.). And so my time here was in some ways more essential, more intensive—we boarders were stuck on campus, subject to the constant pressure and pleasure of its design, with only brief releases to smoke at Denny's, or wander into Detroit or Royal Oak with friends who drove.

I am tempted to go into the main academic building, but I won't. Class is in session, after all.

The boarding school—and here comes another high school girl, walking by, this one at least dressed more warmly—is a place that I associate strongly with both an aesthetic and a sexual awakening. Yes, it sounds dramatic, but since I attended during my teens, the sexual part is obvious. At the risk of sounding like a person I dislike, the girls here were (and are) stunning, which is no surprise considering the amount of money and power and privilege propping each one up. One imagines they spend an exceptional amount of time on appearance, through surgery and makeup, willpower and contortion and exfoliation, so they are works in progress. They are subject to their own pressures, they have a tradition to uphold: they are designed, produced. They are controlled; they show self-control. They are here, contained, they are nearly art, on display for themselves, for all of us. They are at once object and performance, and of course they're more, too, though it's easy to miss what goes on below the gloss, and they are not here for me, except in my most solipsistic and dirty teenage dreams.

The one school is actually two: Cranbrook is the boys' school (mascot: crane), and Kingswood is the girls' (mascot, oddly: aardvark). Students live on separate campuses in rigorously controlled residence halls ensuring that no one gets in the sort of trouble they probably all want to get in. This is the kind of trouble—blissful, confused, hormonal—I wanted here, but not the kind I actually got into.

I have spent the better part of the day as a visiting writer at Cass Tech High School, one of the best public schools in the City of Detroit, about two miles from the city's center and about fifteen miles from Cranbrook (to connect the two, you have to pass by 8 Mile, Eminem-land, subject of the movie and the ghetto mythology slash marketing surrounding him, his rap, and the place). Cass Tech is older than Cranbrook, founded as Cass Union School in 1861, originally to provide training in the trades to young (white) males. Skip almost a century and a half forward, and Cass Tech's students are now almost entirely African American. Teachers buy their own markers, paper. I got the feeling that this is a place where teachers are doing the Good Work, the work that everyone respects, exalts, and talks about: the work that few actually want to do. Yet it is, in its way, a success story. Certainly the students I met were bright and engaged, creative and funny and thinking of college, so that's a good indication. It's housed in a very old and once-beautiful building (allegedly modernized in 1985, though it's hard to see the effects of that—everything here feels used and lived in, ghostly, expired) in the midst of the vision you probably have of Detroit—burned-out hulking post-industrial everything, the trashed grand buildings. Everything without windows. The effects of massive neglect, corruption, and white flight. Racial tension, riots, eroding labor markets: once-boom, now it's all depression. You know this story, as does Michael Moore. Michigan knows this story particularly well.

Cut to Cranbrook: isolated, impeccably kept up, aside from the aesthetically pleasing wear that comes from the bricks' slowly eroding edges that connote graceful age, distinction, and prestige, not neglect, exhaustion, budget cuts—these are managed ruins that require constant upkeep. This place is a near-utopian project: "I would encourage the cultivation of the power of vision—look ahead, aim true . . . I would encourage the determination not to let go to waste the forces of power and genius in boy or girl in any walk of life"—so said George Booth, the creator of Cranbrook schools, in 1924.

What sort of revelation am I expecting? Do I want to witness the convergence of forces that have acted (and continue to act) on me? I am hoping for the slick results of the reconstruction of my past: epiphany, a soliloquy, something that sounds rich, intellectual, and ends in *y*.

I am sitting now in another courtyard (Cranbrook is essentially a long string of courtyards, both physical and metaphorical), this one facing the boys' dorms with the main academic building right behind me. Several guys in sweatshirts and dirty jeans repair the masonry to the sounds of unidentifiable soft rock emanating from a boom box while a couple dozen kids with cell phones walk by, many of them dressed *exactly* the same way (think classic preppy plus a little bit of hip-hop) as they were when I was here. That is, I'm talking about the boys: the girls have updated their look somewhat with the inexplicable pleated skirts that I am seeing everywhere this summer. One guy walks by with an old Lacoste-designed Izod polo (the one with the alligator on it)—clearly a vintage piece.

When I first enrolled at the school, I bought a handful of cardigans from JCPenney, one of the dozen stores in the Copper Country Mall in the small town in the Upper Peninsula of Michigan where I was raised. I wanted, ridiculously, unsurprisingly, to fit in, and thought that meant cardigans. JCPenney is one of the best stores where I am from, which says something about where I am from. I never wore them once. Presumably I threw them away. I think they were made of rayon or something. No one at this school wore cardigans and certainly not the kind you find at JCPenney.

Twelve years ago, I was inside the main academic building with a future ahead of me in computer science or experimental physics, something hard and crunchy, cold and theoretical. When I was kicked out of school here, I returned—ashamed and angry—to my original high school, Houghton High, via interstate then four-lane road narrowing down to two-lane with rare opportunities to pass. It's ten hours away by car, though as the crow flies, it's more like seven; taking the Greyhound bus up from Pontiac, as I did a number of times, makes the trip approximately twenty long bombs of hours, and unbelievably unpleasant; one had to resort to getting drunk on Robitussin to make it even close to passable. When I returned to Houghton I found myself a couple months ahead of my classmates (I had already passed the AP tests), so I finished my high school career in lazy infamy, charged with crimes downstate but not having to do anything school-related, graduating finally—though not from the school I expected—with a high GPA. Colleges, employers value GPAs. They also value graduating.

◆

Twelve years ago, I had not heard of the mathematical subfield of topology—summarized here by the mathematician Leonard Blackburn in an e-mail to me:

Topology is basically a geometric subject (as you probably know). But it is a geometry without shape or measurement. Rather topology deals with other properties of objects that can be described without measurements or specific shapes. You may have heard that a coffee cup is topologically equivalent to a donut. This is true because, shape and measurement aside, they both are a lump of material with one hole through it (the handle in the case of the cup). In other words, the coffee cup (if it were malleable) could be reshaped into the shape of a donut without any breaks or tears in the process. But there is much more to topology than this. Topology also deals with things such as knots, networks, and non-geometric entities such as transfinite ordinal numbers and other mathematical concepts. Topology can be applied to many disciplines including particle physics and psychology.

Today things are different. I know more about topology, about form and connections, connectivity. I know about electronic circuits, how to bend technology to illicit use. This is what topology has to offer us: it is abstract, about electricity or water or anything that flows equally throughout a form, that moves through channels.

My students say that their poems have good "flow." What does that mean, I ask them. What do you know about flow? They are thinking, possibly, of Eminem, the white Detroit face of hip-hop so attractive to the suburban kids. They are thinking of Eminem whose persona is famously (and allegedly) something of a violent disconnect from his regular self. They map their Abercrombie & Fitch lifestyles onto this darker other. This is one method of rebellion, of mapping one kind of life onto another, making a connection to something outside themselves, outside the boundaries of their world. For me, it was wires and phones and computer crime, synth-pop with queer-eye overtones. For me it was breaking into systems, it was listening in to conversations: it was about connection to another darker electronic world.

An axiom is a mathematical statement regarded as self-evidently true, requiring no proof. Whereas a theorem requires a proof. Proof in mathematical terms is more specific and rigorous (like all math terms are) than our real-life versions of proof. Contrary to what we see on *Law & Order* all the time, strong evidence does not equal proof.

Proof has played a central role in my life because of my past relationship with crime. Various proofs can be (have been) deployed, arrayed against me.

◆

I go down to the bookstore where a kid is watching soccer via satellite. One team, improbably, scores, and so they—both player and fan, a hemisphere apart—celebrate by going down on their knees together. There is shrieking. I buy myself a Frappuccino and T-shirts that I will later be too embarrassed to wear because of the questions they will elicit from people who see me on the street. What year did you graduate, they'll ask, and I won't want to tell them my story.

Cranbrook does want me. I am somewhere in the institutional memory. I am on its mailing lists, my name in bits somewhere in the files. They send me form letters and hit me up for money. I don't remind them that I am not much, if anything, of an alum because I like that they haven't figured this out. I am at once within and outside their world. I balance on a paradox, a seam, a line of ore receding into the earth.

After his five-year reunion, my brother (more successful than me at the Cranbrook thing) tells me many of his classmates were doing very well for themselves, which is no surprise. A friend of mine from my sophomore year plays a large role in the Upjohn pharmaceuticals corporation. Now he owns Kalamazoo's minor league hockey team.

This is why I don't like to attend the reunions. Plus I have the secret fear that I will be forcibly ejected. Is it fear or is it desire for this kind of recognition? Maybe I want to threaten all this status, all this stasis: maybe I want to be recognized, ejected, expelled from this world. I felt this way when I was enrolled, too, that I did not belong to this place in the way that others did.

⬤

Most people probably know Cranbrook for the Institute of Art (the art museum) or the Science Museum—the public faces on the idea of the place. The Cranbrook Academy of Art is a prestigious and influential graduate art school. I had no appreciation for this when I went to high school right next door. We called the art students dirty hippies (they did look the part, or so we thought—but what did any of us know about hippies?). We fired water balloons at, or otherwise harassed, them. They were convenient scapegoats, emblems of a strange alternate life, far away from the slick, bright futures we envisioned for ourselves.

Now the art students are closer to my temperament and interests. I am sitting in the Cranbrook Academy of Art's library, which is quite small but beautiful, also Saarinen-designed. This is a place I never entered as a high school student—it was not for us. But the amazing art museum next door was, at least in theory. I only remember venturing in one time: an officially endorsed field trip to see W. S. Merwin read poems about pterodactyls and fossil fuels. This is all that remains with me about that night, this lame image I have held onto for years. That and the passage through the museum to the reading, meaning I have a memory of light and space and destination, but it's hazy now, misshapen, indistinct—it breaks down even as I try to examine it. The museum is closed today. I will have to come back tomorrow if I want to see it.

Although I now prefer the art students to the high schoolers, I don't feel as if I fit in here either. I'm no painter or sculptor; though I do work as a designer, it's nothing radical. Today I accidentally wore Cranbrook colors—khaki pants and a green, blue, and white anorakish item (it's from J.Crew, signifier of lives unlike mine, of the ritzy mall, though I bought it, as I do the majority of my clothes, at the Salvation Army) that has been sitting in the trunk of my car for exercise, but it is cold today, so I put it on. I feel a little too preppy for art, a little too arty for the preppies. (Is it possible that I even wore it today to exhibit a desire to fit in with these kids in the way I did not when I was here twelve years ago? And if so, what does that prove?)

The chairs in the art library are predictably gorgeous: they may well be Saarinen designs (probably Eero Saarinen, the son, the other celebrated Saarinen designer). Everything is bright and subdued and beautiful. The whole place says Arts & Crafts. There are huge and unwieldy books (one title, as an example: *A. Essenwein, Pfarrkirche Z. Heil Gereon in Köln*) stacked on shelves that are labeled "Rare Books: Fragile—Do Not Touch." I am seriously tempted to touch one just to see if anyone will intervene.

◆

Some Evidence—a Short List of Ander Monson's Criminal History at Cranbrook Schools: breaking and entering; shoplifting; stealing master keys and security radios; rerouting and rewiring of a number of phones; switching a professor's home phone with the pay-phone line resulting in a semester's worth of free calls and a befuddled professor; illegally using a phone line then for illegal activity re: Comerica Bank, re: Unix Systems, re: Shell access, resulting in revocation of telephone privileges, and later wire-splicing, duct-taping around this problem; allegedly drinking; using father's credit cards to buy way too much stuff (sorry, Dad); using stolen credit cards to charge Ozzy Osbourne tickets for a friend; stealing blank checks then used by not-bright friend to order pizza; using stolen phone cards; electronic breaking and entering numerous fucking times; being accused of smoking inside a dorm room (the only time Monson was actually suspended, and by the way he was not smoking but was with someone who was—a rare moment of innocence in this otherwise criminal wash).

In my life, there is a tension between shame and pride in recollecting my criminal past. I can't avoid it. I am proud of these transgressions. They are like babies, Coppertoned and chipper in the sun. I like to shine them up like trophies and put them on my shelf, bring them down for parties to entertain my guests. Dance, motherfuckers! Spin, show off for me! They are what I've done, whatever claim I have to glory or ignominy. Simultaneously, I'm aware that they are (I am) also quite dumb. These acts have affected others—family, teachers, friends, who have worried, have been forever sorry on my behalf. I'm not exactly penitent, nor am I flat-out apologetic. I am again standing on a seam, possibly a scam. I am glad to have gone through the experiences, to have come out the other side. In one version of my life, I could have ended up in jail, become a completely different story (my life as Choose Your Own Adventure: if you go left, please turn to page 37; if you go right, keep reading). I was arrested and punished while still technically a juvenile, and that makes a difference. Have You Ever Been Convicted of a Felony? Having to answer yes to all those college and job-application questions would have produced a very different result. I hold these stories close to my chest because they did not lance me, bring me down.

Today I am looking for connections—both my own to the place and to my questionable past, and between myself and the body of knowledge that informs the design of the place; I am looking for connectivity and resistance to transformation, both in history and in the here and now. In what ways did I resist Cranbrook? In what ways did I give in? How am I responsible? What does that even mean? Was it—this history of my acting out, my now-obvious rebellion—because of my mother's death when I was seven? And if it is, who cares? Why do I want connections? For resolution? For revolution? How much guilt am I supposed to feel?

Psychology is tied into topology too, with its interest in the Gestalt, in maps, and neural nets, and projections, connections between psychological dynamics: these sorts of cognitive phenomena. Working at connections is working at the self and the way it works or does not work. I am trying hard to think about this place, and my place in it, in topological terms.

❦

Cranbrook and I are discontinuous. Certainly this is true, physically. I am not literally part of the architecture of the place, nor am I in residence on its campus.

Educationally or philosophically, it's a different story. Although I did not graduate from the school, they can take credit for me in some ways, that is, I feel that I am a product of my education here, which emphasized liberal thinking, excellence, well-roundedness, interests in interdisciplinary work, and an appreciation for aesthetics and culture. And in my expulsion from the school, I am continuous with the genre of Boarding-School Lit., which appreciates a thrilling suspension and expulsion. The results in my case were different, though: I didn't have money and influence to fall back on, the safety net of privilege that allows for the entertaining stories of boarding-school hijinks to remain entertaining. And even in my expulsion (the twins *suspension* and *expulsion*—being held at a length temporarily above or from a place and being pushed permanently away—both give weight to the power of place to shape us, and we also shape, take part in, places; think physics, that any action has an equal and opposite reaction), I have proceeded out in a definite trajectory from it; that is, I am expelled from Cranbrook (my own private Idaho, my beautiful half-assed Eden) as it has accelerated me away from it. I have also put a nick in it, exerted some equal and opposite (if minor) force upon it. And I am trying to tally up that force right here. I can trace myself back to it, or I can at least try.

Physics, what I thought would be my chosen field of study, is all about the recognition and calculation of the forces that act upon bodies at any given time. If we can identify a body and the forces that have acted upon it over time, we can trace the body back.

That sounds a lot like a metaphor.

Eliel Saarinen, primary architect of the place, was Finnish. Where I am from in Upper Michigan there are a lot of Finns—the street signs in the town where my parents live are titled in both Finnish and English. Finlandia University (see their surprisingly popular hats that read: *F U*), formerly Suomi College, is the only private university in Upper Michigan; it is one of the only schools in America to offer a full major in the Finnish language. I have long disliked the Finns—those who immigrated from a cold and isolated place to a new cold and isolated place probably felt at home in the long winters here; those who mapped their lives onto a new landscape. It's not rational or defensible, I know (I am after all a quarter-Finnish), but it is as if they brought me into Michigan and left me here. There were so many of them, and all of them related, and often they seemed nuts. More likely I was looking for some kind of door to kick in, vandalize, and they were easy, blond targets. But then the Finns are responsible for much beauty, too, this Saarinen-led heritage of grand design, this Cranbrook connection.

●

The more I wander around campus, the more I realize two things—first, just how much of this whole place is *designed*. Everywhere you go, there is evidence of control—even walking through the dozens of trails that connect the boys' and girls' schools across the 315 acres of the campus, I run across dozens of concrete pools that are connected by a network of aqueducts and spouts. Water flows down forty short tiers into a pool, is then funneled underneath the walking path to collect in another concrete pool, which then empties downward into a wilder area (a swamp of some sort), and I suspect that even the wild area is intentional in its wildness. Every twig feels fraught with intention.

Second, I realize how much of this place I actually *remember* now, even a dozen years later, walking the trails I haven't walked in over a decade and marveling at the places only accessible by walking—the old Greek Theatre, for instance, where I never saw anyone I didn't bring with me. I remember thinking to myself when I was a student that most other students could not appreciate the beauty of the place in the way that I did. I felt somehow that this place was meant for me alone—or that I, among the many, had discovered it. This suggests a couple of things about me, primarily my (former—?) arrogance and solipsism, but it also points to the first time I felt as though I was having an aesthetic experience.

I expect that this is the exact effect that the designers were going for—offering the pleasure of discovery to individuals by tucking these places away from casual inspection. The place—like art, like mathematics, language, literature, and maybe even like those Kingswood girls—rewards your investigation, yields secrets to your unbroken gaze. Even Cranbrook itself is nearly invisible in the context of the larger city- and suburb-clutter—the only real evidence when you drive by on Woodward are two signs, instances of good typography (a hallmark of the Cranbrook School of Design) and a hilly entrance with a security gate. You have to want to find it, and the school does not make this easy. The gate means exclusivity, privilege, scarcity. Think of it in terms of economics.

This is turning into a sort of theorem: Cranbrook offers a designed aesthetic experience in order to produce a certain kind of student, person, aesthete, citizen.

This production process is not immediately obvious or immediately effective.

—

If Cranbrook has a theorem, so does Cass Tech. What kind of students is Cass Tech designed to produce, and what students does it actually produce? This has to do with shape, topology, again, sets of dynamics operating on individuals. What *is* a school? Where is the heart of Cass Tech? Is the school the project in the middle of the projects? Is it the building? The students, who succeed in spite of, or in honor of, the building and the place? Success can be rebellion. Is it the teachers? I talked for a while with the teacher of the class I visited. She was tired. We talked writing: she was an aspiring science-fiction writer, was working on a novel. She had been reassigned to this school midyear after her position was cut at another school. She, like others, wouldn't be here very long. As she walked me out through the gloom of the greenish halls, she shrugged, said they were going to have a new building next year, at least she hoped they would. Exiting the building I wasn't sure what my experience was supposed to have been, or what it was—expectation mapped onto the actual, somehow creating experience. Ostensibly I was brought in so urban students could interact with writers, discover their creative sides, go on to represent their family, their school, their city in literary prose. Maybe the flip side was that writers would get to interact with urban students and take something back with them. I took back the image of the building and the image of the city as related to history, as related to my history with school, with Cranbrook. They brought me into the center of the city from the Lake Michigan side of the state, a couple hours away, and then I left it for the other story of the suburbs and my past.

If this were a nicer (or a weekend) day, I would have probably run into more alumni wandering the grounds. When I was a student here, the only people I ever saw on the trails were either art students or alumni, drawn back into the place in search of memory or something, trying to fit their cognitive maps of remembered Cranbrook to the actual Cranbrook, which does not seem to have changed much (surely this is the designer's intention), wandering its shady conduits and sharing it with their partners, spouses, or whatever.

It is both creepy and wonderful that I remember the curlicuing trails, the Greek Theatre, all the lovely tiered reflecting pools, and unsettlingly naked statues that dot the grounds. This is a testament both to my own aesthetic experience of the place as well as the efficacy of its design. Thus: I am a product of this place. Or: I am an individual who was formed by the place. This is one kind of proof.

One more note on the Greek Theatre while I am here: this is one of few places on campus where you can hear cars. Silence—the experience of insulation from the ring and clamor of the city—is mostly absolute at Cranbrook. The theatre is close enough to one of the roads that lead through the many mansions of Bloomfield Hills that you can actually hear traffic. I wonder about this flaw in the design. And then I notice flaw number two. One of the bas-reliefs on the wall of the theatre has representations of frolicking Greeks in the midst of some bacchanal. There are two children depicted among the adults, one of them (is he playing a lyre or a lute? I never know the difference) has lost one of his original carved stone legs, so instead of the leg, there is a midthigh amputation with two steel rods sticking out that were once meant to anchor the concrete in and prevent this very thing from happening, and that now are simply disturbing—this is a flaw too, I think, and a telling one considering my own interest in limblessness and amputation. This place has made me, is in turn made for me.

❧

Topology is concerned with notions of stability, proximity, and shape.

Cranbrook is concerned with notions of stability. The administration tries to avoid negative media attention, which of course I brought to them (*see* the *Detroit Free Press* circa my arrest). I suspect this was the reason I was finally expelled.

Cranbrook is all about architectural design, which is *foremost* about stability, about the persistence of form and substance over time against gravity, stress, and erosion. It is secondarily about aesthetics, though aesthetics always gets first billing until the construction collapses, and then we turn with questions to the engineers.

Cranbrook is concerned with notions of shape, at least in its devotion to aesthetics and form. The metaphors of the school are forming, shaping (I realize I am eliding the semantic jump here from mathematics to linguistics) their students. Their students wrap their hands around wet and spinning clay in the ceramics studio. They are forming with their hands. At night, in dorm rooms or on the walking trails around the Greek Theatre, students embrace, doing the same: forming, being formed.

There are other metaphors that could be deployed as proof of this.

Then there's proximity, a connection to psychology: the law of proximity, a principle of organization in Gestalt psychology, holds that objects or events near to one another in space or time are perceived as belonging together as a unit. So by talking about Cranbrook and Cass Tech in an essay, one begins to bring them together. Cranbrook and I are in proximity, too, and therefore we are one. The same goes for the relation between the self and the other, the present and the past, the criminal and the sexual. And so on. Proximity is one method by which we discern or create meaning in the relations between things.

❧

I sit in another courtyard facing Cranbrook House, the admissions center, the centerpiece of the place, and look past yet another spurting cherub fountain. Beyond this fountain is one more fountain heading up a long reflecting pool, leading up to a set of stairs, which leads up to the house—this fountain too has a figure, this one a man with what I believe to be a lyre. It looks like a small harp, right? If that's the case, then my previous lyre was almost definitely a lute. Did I learn nothing in my classes here?

The daffodils are blooming in spite of the cold. I have a vague memory of a graduation slash prom-night party at this mansion that I was explicitly (?—I have done my part to isolate myself from some of the trappings of privilege that came along with my education, so this may be a faulty memory, badly in need of repair, a memory attached to a storm system of doubt) not invited to. I'm not sure what to make of this now.

Right beneath the House (between the House and the lake as you walk down) is an alcove that faces Kingswood, the girls' school, directly. I remember this overlook as one of my two favorite places (the Greek Theatre being the other): it felt like I was even more of an outsider here, boy at the girls' school, on the edge of another mystery. Here a hidden alcove reveals a statue of a naked young woman with one more fountain behind her. Someone has placed a daffodil in one of her open hands. One of these two things must be a metaphor.

Oh no! A further revelation: in her other hand—invisible from where I was sitting initially, but visible when I got up to move—is an apple (the apple, unlike the flower, is part of the actual sculpture).

We learned about juxtaposition in my sophomore-year English class.

I hear girls' voices echo across the lake. I see what appears to be an actual crane on the water among several honking geese. I don't think I've ever seen a live crane before.

—

Theorem: Aside from the administration and their actions, Cranbrook Schools are Good.

Proof Sketch: Anecdotal, accumulating, accompanied by synth-pop and sobs.

1. I am sitting in my dorm room, midway between dejection and anger, in the week I have been asked to leave Cranbrook when my AP calculus class shows up. Maybe Depeche Mode is playing on my stereo. The class comes to my door to give me

their support. I am moved. Some of them, I think (or hope, perhaps) show evidence of tears.

2. My parents are angry of course—they foresee a prison future, a high-school-dropout future, and expensive lawyer action requiring money that we probably do not have. Either they or I cry on the phone or after, probably both.

3. Sophomore year. The dean and a straight-up guy whom all the students respect hugely, is deposed, is forced to step down from his position. It was never clear what had happened, except that he did not want this. I remember him breaking down in front of the boarding students who had gathered in one of the ornate rooms for a dorm meeting. While he was an administrator (and was thus regarded with suspicion), he was the only administrator who seemed like an actual, honest person. I liked him a great deal. The director of the residence halls at the time would take over the position. It felt like a coup d'état. We had just learned those words in class.

4. After I am expelled from the school three months before graduation, and well after college applications are due, and after I've received full scholarships to schools such as Rice and Case Western Reserve, Cranbrook informs all the schools to which I have applied that I was expelled. They revoke my scholarships (and, in some cases, my actual admission). I attend Michigan Technological University, where my father teaches, for a year, and then I reapply. My family's angry, and there is lawsuit talk. But my brother still attends the school, and we feel that a lawsuit might be held against him. As it is he goes on to graduate and become president of the senior class. My expulsion and the rumors that surround it probably contribute to his popularity. No one cries in this anecdote.

5. One of the trips back up to my family in the Upper Peninsula is on the bus. I have been given a mix tape by my friend Erin, whom I had loved for years in my own way, whom I was now leaving permanently behind. I am listening to it on the way back up—this trip a model for, an abstract of, my eventual expulsion. I remember Morrissey, and a song by Coro & Teleesa, a cover of Springsteen's "Because the Night" featur-

ing samples from Depeche Mode's "Master and Servant," a song very much about assuming and abdicating control. I am thinking here of love and loss and the possibility of streaks of tears, and not of crime, psychosexual dynamics that I can only map out in retrospect.

6. Cranbrook Schools traditionally dominate Michigan high-school hockey. They give a lot of scholarships to get talented players from all across the country. These scholarships are "academic" since they can't actually award athletic scholarships. Some of the athletes are good students. Another recent power in high-school hockey is Calumet, Michigan, a small former mining town in the Upper Peninsula. Calumet plays host to Cranbrook's hockey team circa 1994 on a long road trip just before the state playoffs. Although I played for much of my life and went to many college hockey games during my childhood, before leaving for Cranbrook, at this point I had not gone to one for years. I did go to this game—such a good story: small town versus big money. The game is excellent, and I am completely transfixed by the atmosphere of tension and aggression: by the surge of the third period I am no longer living in my head, at least for twenty more minutes; Calumet wins. I am elated. Someone in the crowd screams a fuck you to my former private school. I assure you that no one here is listening to Erasure. My interest in the sport—in sport itself—is reignited. It's as if I've just reconciled with a long-lost and aggressive member of my family, my pissed-off blood. I wanted to burn things just then. If I was less self-conscious, I might have cried.

―

From the perspective of the juvenile delinquent, topology, or at least topography, is very important—both at Cranbrook and elsewhere. For me, access was a key element of my school experience. Through due diligence and theft, I got my hands on master keys to all the buildings. I had a set of two-way security radios, industrial-looking, made by Motorola. I wanted to extend the campus out as far as I could. We were not allowed phones in our rooms, so I spliced into several of the main phone lines and ran cords into my room—I had this thought of myself as a nexus, as connected by thousands of physical, electric conduits to the world, information flowing up to and through me: it was very cyberpunk. In any place there are proscribed areas, and to certain personalities this of course presents a challenge, irresistible—Conrad's blank spaces on the map.

For students, the geographical boundaries of the campus cannot be breached without consequence—one must sign in and out and list a destination. And no overnights without approval via telephone or fax from home.

Form is defined by boundary. You know this, I am sure.

How much mathematics is too much mathematics? I don't want to punch you with it into submission.

Most of the students there lived without boundaries, whether this entailed the money their parents donated to the school to keep their kid from being expelled, or the simple fact of moneyed life and the privilege it brings. Another friend of mine whose family (like the earlier example) had made their fortune, possibly, in pharmaceuticals is very unhappy now. Exceptionally talented at anything he tried (he taught himself—from scratch, no piano knowledge whatsoever—to play "Rhapsody in Blue"), he now cannot commit to anything at all, and stalemates himself in Hawaii.

My parents did not have millions to endow a scholarship or support the construction of a building. I don't even wish they had. I can't imagine the dullness, uselessness of a life without the aegis of constraint, without space breaks, ending sentences, and thoughts of higher mathematics.

◦

More rushing water. Much bamboo and topiary precision. The Oriental Garden is gorgeous, but by this point I'm nearly saturated with beauty and control—this is like the diminishing returns of visiting each additional cathedral in Europe after your mind has been wrecked by the first three.

What thesis have I set out to prove? What thesis have I proved?

I am trying to find ways to map my experience of the place onto the place itself. How do these two things converge?

◦

I do not know what to make of this. Again, outside the girls' school (this time on the school side of the lake), I'm sitting on a promenade that juts out into the water. Directly above me is a statue of two young and naked women. They are gallivanting together—no wrestling or hot oil, of course (this isn't Cinemax or Hooters, sorry) but they are semisensuously holding hands. I'm not sure the sculptor was going for this, but it reads as hot. The quality of the sculpted breasts suggests implants, actually, from their size and buoyancy, though that seems unlikely given the age of the sculpture—how strange our culture is in our attempts to approximate received ideas of form, form that resists age and the passage of time, form that resists the natural tendency toward decay.

This overt sexuality is getting creepy—or maybe it is just me; of course it is me, but it's also (the mostly male end of) society: Google "schoolgirl" and "sex" and you get one and a half million hits. That's quite the po-mo porno sprawl. Surely there's something here about sexual imprinting in the teenage years and a permanent fixation? There's undoubtedly some sort of synaptic pathway formed during adolescence that might, that must, explain this phenomenon, our collective tendencies toward the perverse, the pursuit of the forbidden.

Walking, I've come across a jogger. Now there is a connection between the physical form and the development of the aesthetic. Beautiful bodies, beautiful minds, corresponding exterior and interior.

The grounds here are beautiful too, of course, though cold.

Correction on the crane: it is a swan. Other birds go honking quickly overhead.

Whereas Cranbrook houses math, science, computer science, etc., the Kingswood buildings house the English courses, and all the visual arts (high-school students don't get to interface with the graduate students at the art academy). Surely this split is a holdover from old gender stereotypes, but the simple fact of the buildings still remains—and Cranbrook is a school best known for its art, its literature. Its literary magazine, obnoxiously titled *Gallimaufry* (meaning: a hodgepodge, jumble, or confused medley; originally: a hash of various kinds of meats) has a large yearly budget, bigger than most professional literary magazines. The production values are of course through the roof. As I didn't go in much for art or literature when I was here, I don't think I've ever owned a copy.

Students take courses on both campuses—they commute between and connect two geographies. Plus every student here is at once occupying this physical place and the place they come from, their home topography, and the topographies of their dreams, their future lives. The students in this posh place want the mythology of the streets, maybe to live vicariously, maybe as rebellion. The school wants control. It does not allow hip-hop-styled clothes, T-shirts, thongs, bare midriffs, loose pants that expose boxers or briefs. Students wear collared shirts and slacks, skirts for girls, ties for boys. I wore the worst ties I could find, polyester, garish, seventies, and explosive, and I once wore three ties simultaneously, working within the dress code but against it, impressing no one. These students want their jacked-up Escalades, their rides pimped; they want the streets, they want Detroit, even as they don't want to be in Detroit unless they're driving through on their way to a concert downtown or the Super Bowl.

The proximity of these two things is a useful juxtaposition: the often-polished gem of Cranbrook and the nearly scuttled ship of Detroit. The contrast strengthens both extremes.

I am trying to make maps—topographic, aesthetic, criminal, sexual, adolescent—of the place as I remember it.

What am I waiting for—what sort of revelation about the place would satisfy me, would satisfy you? I am sitting in the designed world of the campus expecting it to tell me something, to suggest a response to it. I want something beyond the uneasy response of the body's arousal—that doesn't wash with me as epiphany.

What will it take as proof to convince me, to connect these dots into something beautiful and continuous? Is everything disjunction, scattered Legos, logos, random blips and dots? What will remain after all the detritus has washed, has been cleared finally away?

That you should know, in other words, that it [the text of *Let Us Now Praise Famous Men*] has no part in the realm where disbelief is habitually suspended. It is much simpler than that. It is simply an effort to use words in such a way that they will tell as much as I want to and can make them tell of a thing which happened and which, of course, you can have no other way of knowing. It is in some degree worth your knowing what you can of [it] not because you have any interest in me but simply as the small part it is of human experience in general. It is one way of telling the truth: the only possible way of telling the kind of truth I am here most interested to tell. (James Agee, *Let Us Now Praise Famous Men*)

I first read James Agee when I was at Cranbrook. In particular, we read *A Death in the Family* in English class my junior year—the year we learned about epiphany and juxtaposition, the literature of masturbation, and Joyce—with Mr. W., a very intelligent and drunken man, and I do not remember the book at all. The irony is not lost on me that what I am trying to describe—this sensory and now increasingly fraught and intellectual recollection of the place—is not in any way similar to the Southern tenant sharecroppers that Agee, increasingly fraught, increasingly frustrated with the impossibility of his project, increasingly aware of his body and its sexual responses, describes in the quote above. So there is nothing of the grand social project here in this essay (though there is in the design, the tiny utopia of the campus itself), and I don't want to draw comparisons between *Let Us Now . . .* and this text because my essay clearly will not hold up its end. But the kernel is there: this is another fraction of human experience, one that most people do not have access to. Hence—and even while I am trying to churn it up, to make something golden out of it—I am beholden to the place, and the memory of the place. I am held captive by my experience and my subsequent expulsion.

There's the Eden echo here again, our conceptions of aesthetic perfection and our expulsion from it.

Is this grandiose? Is it really grandiose? How I have always loved the grandiose.

Crime is aesthetically appealing. It is one of the great contemporary subjects of media inquiry and literature—an excellent and puzzling set of transgressions, alternately explicable by social-science theories, economics, psychology, and cultural study. Crime can be an aesthetic performance—a press against the boundaries we set for ourselves. My crime was a performance (and is a performance now, here, for you): I was performing for my friends, for the Kingswood girls, for my parents, for the administration and my teachers (this was how I distinguished myself). And I performed this one part well. When the Michigan State Computer Crime Task Force raided my room in my senior year, they told me (a friend of mine—busted weeks before, I had just found out—had fingered me) that I was the ringleader of some kind of hacker group. They were *taking me down* (their words—really). They supposed I was deposed.

Crime, violence is fascinating. *See also* John Woo, Sergio Leone, Elmore Leonard, Quentin Tarantino, the eternal verities of *Law & Order*.

I was ringleader of nothing—there was no ring, and I was not at its center. At best they were searching for a satisfying pattern, like the patterns you see on TV and in the movies. It's true that I was friends with a couple dozen people who were perpetrating different computer crimes throughout my teenage years, but in no way did I lead anyone or anything. I went by the handle "The Grim Reaper," which I got from somewhere, possibly one too many games of *Dungeons & Dragons,* or my performances as death-metal aficionado, flipping through the stacks at the awful Musicland (now Sam Goody, still awful) in the tiny Copper Country Mall, looking for the most obnoxious band names (Cannibal Corpse ranks pretty high, as does Lawnmower Deth) and song titles ("Seventh Church of the Apocalyptic Lawnmower," the classic "Satan's Trampoline," and "Maim, Mower, Maim," to iterate a few gems). The metal band (I hesitate to grant them either term) Grim Reaper is impossibly and awesomely lame by comparison to real death metal (a sort of third-rate Iron Maiden at best), but there's the possibility that I thought it looked cool. I even had my black (of course) Land's End bag monogrammed *TGR,* which I had to explain, to my immediate discredit, for many years thereafter. I had my avatar, my persona, to maintain.

●

Theorem: Maybe this—my criminal and educational history, my life—is in the end about control, about understanding limits, running my finger along any boundary I could find.

1. Crime is about control and power. Given laws, the criminal transgresses, creates a kind of internal locus of control. How

can we not love transgression? It demonstrates limits. It reassures the rest of us, safely within the circle.

2. Boarding school is about both of these things—rules, procedures, and punishments in a closed domestic system designed to keep the subjects safe, which also means under control.

3. Mathematics takes control as a given: it is a perfect created system—it is designed, each theorem and postulate subject to rigorous standards of proof—and its workings do not bow to the sloppy unexpectedness of the real world.

4. Although, consider Gödel's Incompleteness Theorem, which suggests that all mathematical systems must be logically and eventually incomplete.

5. I am attracted to math, to that kind of formal play, to the idea of definitive proof, and I like the idea of Gödel's black hole waiting there for us.

6. The Grim Reaper is always in control; he stands on very edge of what we have. Or is that just a convenient fiction?

7. I also like the idea of design: I do book covers, web design, typography. I've handset type for letterpresses, letter after letter, manually adjusting the letterspacing with tiny slips of copper, the leading with slim strips of lead (this is where we get the word *leading*). When I took the letterpress-printing class I told my instructor that I really wanted to print a broadside in my own blood. He was horrified and maybe a little bit entertained because I think he laughed. I could probably come up with a hundred examples like this.

8. Control invites rebellion. Rules suggest their own fracture.

9. *See also* NWA, "Fuck Tha Police" from *Straight Outta Compton,* a tape I might have shoplifted from Musicland in the Copper Country Mall, and I remember white kids at Cranbrook—quasi-thuggy proto-gangstas—blasting this song from their British-Racing-Green Eddie-Bauer-package Ford Explorers, and my friend George attempting to blast it from his anemic bedside clock radio, as we all watched the thing just give up, the bass separating, becoming click and hiss and static.

10. I stopped shoplifting when I turned seventeen. Something got through to me, or I got through to it, a new place where I was just beyond that.

11. How can I prove anything about my life? How can I even see it? I'm not sure lives make any kind of sense in the present tense, and maybe not even in retrospect, when seen from space and a hundred years of context. Still I want to shake it, kiss it, and release it, see where it lands.

12. I dream sometimes that I am totally, improbably, in control. It is a lie I have believed on and off throughout my life. It's safe, appealing. But then: how dull. It would be like what the uninitiated imagine math to be—ordered, neat, rows of equations stretching out forever in perfect lines, a discovered country. It would be unmoving. Like death, the end of the ghost of intention.

13. I don't like to think about this too much.

◆

I've always been fascinated with the sound and sight of shattering glass. I have been responsible for much of it myself: smashing windows in abandoned buildings (that dot my hometown just as they dot Detroit—Detroit a sort of huge analogue of Upper Michigan, all the peeling varnish and vanished industry, glass so shattered you can't believe its eventual reconstruction), in wrecked cars abandoned in fields, in Michigan Bell trucks. And I have thrown or hit baseballs through neighbors' windows, sometimes apologizing, sometimes not. There is something in the reduction of the smooth uninterrupted composite into the tiny fragments. Continuity and discontinuity. Glass and its transparency—it's there and not. It does not contain light at all, nor fire (for long). It's pressurized and superheated sand, the kind of sand that armors all the nice lake beaches, customized forever for tourists, in Upper Michigan.

And then there's *stampsand,* the darker brother of sand, big black poisonous grit left after rock containing iron ore or copper is processed. There are huge mounds and plains of it all around my hometown. Ten years ago the city dumped a bunch of topsoil on top of the stampsand plains and sold these newly lovely lakefront lots for lots and lots of money. My parents bought one, were planning to build a house. They had to bring in dump-truckloads of dirt, dig huge holes, and fill them in with the good soil in order to plant trees. It was all surface, with a darker other underneath. The land has been reclaimed from its former devastation, albeit with constraints. They owned for a while (and then finally sold six years ago, giving up on the idea) exactly six inches of green rind atop a hundred feet of wreck. Stampsand fused becomes a kind of glass, too, but black, opaque.

Glass is form, control. I love how it reflects, how it refracts, how it shapes and controls fluid, gas, how it is unified and clean and sheer and strong, shaped, though it can be broken. We use it for graduated cylinders. Beakers. Pipettes. Good science things. I am sad to see pop bottles now made of futuristic plastic, which lacks mystique. Glass is losing ground to new polymers, is becoming anachronism, the past tense of technology. I took this nouveau plastic so-called Unbreakable Comb from my barbershop when I was ten. I worked for weeks at this thing, bent it and bent it, and it finally gave, stretched and weakened, whitened, but mostly kept its former form. In the end I took it apart with a hacksaw I took from my dad's toolshed and called it *broken*.

Who am I kidding? Crime, my crime, plays a leading role in this essay. It is the hook herein—the way my life can gather interest.

My criminal career lacked grace. I stumbled through open electronic backdoors, destroyed windows with center punches, stole equipment, rewired phone boxes, fooled pay phones into believing quarters had been inserted. Studies in risk and asininity.

Moments in this five-year-long stumble were transformed into beauty, though.

It did have a narrative arc—rising action, complication, setbacks, increasing risk, and climax and denouement, dethronement. Maybe this is a kind of reckoning, a continued long-term echo or reflection.

❧

To return to the bust, my apprehension, and the end of one of my lives, another anecdote, a proof: We lived in dorms, of course. We had rules: no TVs or phones or refrigerators. No appliances, really. My last spring break at Cranbrook was spent in the Greek half of Cyprus, where I remember breaking away from my family for an afternoon and watching a pornographic film in a cheap theatre there and trying to steal a small television from the place, getting caught, and making some excuse to get away (most likely I tried to cry but couldn't)—and the TV wouldn't even have worked back in the States, since we have different voltages here, so why did I want to steal it? Many of my actions seem inexplicable to me now except in psychiatric terms that don't mean much, really: acting out, projection, internalized anger, the biological processes of clinical depression. While in Cyprus, I called illegally using a device known as a red box (a RadioShack auto-dialer, originally designed to memorize hundreds of phone numbers for users, but modified to reproduce the tone produced when you put a quarter into a pay phone—this of course in the pre–cell-phone, text-messaging world) back to the States to talk with my friend George, and he gave me the heads up that I was busted, that I was seriously fucked. I still had three vacation days in Cyprus to anticipate the ruin of my life—that arc quickly flatlining into a future I did not want.

When I returned to Cranbrook, the lock on my dorm room had been changed. I went around to the window to see all of my possessions mounded on the floor—relocated from the walls and bed and closet into a shapeless mass, an unfortunate instance of controlled entropy—with the carbon copy of a search warrant positioned like a cherry right on the top. In retrospect it was a nice presentation—someone clearly took pleasure in the design of it, my ruination. My computer, of course, was missing, as was all of my pornography and all of my music, the majority of my books, and anything else that the Feds felt like confiscating. I eventually got most of it back, excluding a Wilson Phillips CD that I probably should not have owned, that one of the Task Force members' daughters must have wanted. (The truth of these property seizures is that they take whatever they want from you, since you have so little to leverage for their return.) *Dear Federal Computer Crime Task Force,* I wrote, *you can keep the CD, but please return my pornography,* for I was obsessed with the female form—a rudimentary aesthetic experience).

The story starts to collapse from here—all these balls a couple sentences from crashing to the floor, announcing my failure or my fraud, whichever you prefer—and it ends with seven felony convictions (possession of credit-card information), really by far the least (and least interesting) of my many teenage insurrections. It is on my record still, both at Cranbrook schools and sealed alive in that *Juvenile-Record* grave. I am stamped with it, marked and expelled by it, my trajectory affected at least in part by it, this pushing off from the bounds and rules of the civilization I was privileged to be part of and party to, and in the process I was made, I was manufactured, formed and spit out into the world, sort of nude, teenaged, and angry, through the motions of my own hands and eyes and lips. When I left the Cranbrook gates for the final time, when I was escorted officially off the campus, and the place was free of me and my undirected anger; when I saw the place diminish in the rearview mirror, reflected through the rear window of my parents' Aerostar, and finally become swallowed up by the rest of suburban Detroit, which gave way slowly to the abandoned countryside surrounding I-75, the only freeway that even makes a dent in the wilderness of the Upper Peninsula, and then finally is subsumed by loneliness and evergreens and a terminal case of snow, I was thinking nothing rational, and this is a blank space on my map: I don't remember the trip back up to my home, and while I'm sure it was uncomfortable to say the least for my father, stepmother, and for me, no detail of the thing, my ascent back into the North, and my descent from the moneyed Utopia, remains. It is as a vapor trail, diffused slowly into sky—possible to reconstruct only if you believe in the deterministic universe, the universe as a colossal machine, every force and reaction potentially knowable and understandable, provided that we had the impossible computing power to crunch those numbers.

More recent science tells us that this view of the world is wrong, is anachronism, went out with the convenient mathematics of Newton. Or, that is, it works for most of us who can't deal with the intricacies of quantum theory, relativity, and all that filigree and shadow. But under close observation, it breaks down, everything breaks down, and the world—the atomic world, and thus the whole shebang—must be understood differently, if it can be understood at all.

INDEX FOR X AND THE ORIGIN OF FIRES

A

A brother, a radio, a winter full of snow and thoughts on Liz my X, if she were real or corporeal, if she were more than ghost of truth, if she could be here with me.

A clarinet melody line impressed in wax found in a sleeve above the mantel. Dad's Benny Goodman. Dad's high-school clarinet encased forever in the felt.

A foot going through a rotting wood deck. All the way up to the groin. This particular detail is particularly true.

A list of compelling, gradually compiling evidence.

A moving, morbid feeling.

A protagonist. Do they exist in fiction, in nonfiction. Do they exist in life. Do we need another hero.

Absence. Anger at mine or hers, at anyone's. A block. A way around.

Alibi and alias: everyone generates their own, is their own. We have names and some sort of permanence and halos left behind like salt rings in a sauna.

Always goes without.

Amalgamation. Accumulation. What comes down in time through lines accretes.

An anecdote: I'd destroy any Matchbox cars my dad got for me. Pretend they were the bomb squad and take the hammer to them. Then put them in a can and bury them when I had enough. Ask my dad for more. He'd hold my hand when we went to the store to pick them out. The wax on the floor glistened. Did he hold my brother's hand. Was there a hand to hold.

An anecdote, reconstructed:
     after prom with Liz—after
     prom with Liz with stream-
     ers torn down from the new
     school gym, mementos of
     the dance. Liz and Jesse as
     friends, not dates. On their
     way out to Gay, Michigan,
     where the after-party was. Saw
     something in the road. Not
     drinking, talking. Listening to
     Cowboy Junkies. Some light
     in the car from those they
     passed. Still ice on the ground
     of course up here in spring.
     More light leaking out from
     the fluorescence on his watch
     as he checks it because his
     Toyota's clock does not work.
     He slides the sunroof open so
     Liz can see the moon, so she
     can be happy. Cigarette light
     in passing cars. Dashboard's
     low emissions. Starlight: very
     old. An occasional streetlamp
     or jack-o'-lantern out of
     season on a porch. Candles lit
     inside. A premonition of fire,
     upcoming accident, and fires
     lit forever in response.

An eye for the crucial bit of
     evidence.

Any fragment is an art, an arti-
     fact. Is an echo of the whole. Is
     an echo; is the whole.

Any kind of solace.

Any kind of story.

Anything you give me I will take.

Anything you want to tell me.

Auster, Paul, as existential avatar.

Ballistics.

Blood,
     age of stains
     alcohol
     as embedded in eyes
     as evidence, insufficient or
          sufficient
     as metaphor
     as narrator
     as representative of ego
     as representative of teeth
     collection, for alcohol analysis
     copper content of
     crystal tests for
     distinction of source
     distribution patterns
     enzyme markers
     groups,
          inheritance of
     hemoglobin variants
     importance of,
          to the criminal investigation,
          to the human body,
          to the whole wide breathing,
               bleeding world

loss of, and desperation
omission of evidence in order
    to conceal crimes
on hands,
    removal of by aggravated
        washing
    removal of by amputation
    removal of by any neces-
        sary means
    removal of by "Out! Out!
        Damned Spot"
    removal of in order to
        sleep again
    removal of in order to
        dream of smashing
        glass again
presence of
protein factors
species origin of
spectroscopic tests for
testing equipment
tests, catalytic,
    interference with
    sensitivity of
where from
where to
you know you want it, want to
    see it everywhere.

Bluebells clustered around
    a telephone pole. The tele-
    phone pole adjoined by a
    junction box. The box
    opened and all the connec-
    tions numbered and labeled
    inside. This is a kind of
    beauty in connection.

Brother, a hoot and a bother,
    importance of
    phenomenon of
    relation to danger,
        to events
        to fire
        to light
        to Liz
        to locks
        to mother
        to radio
        to Sault Ste. Marie
        to sinking
        to snowmobiles
        to tools
        to true events
    stigmata
    truth in telling
    truth of, questionable
    wanting things for
    whereabouts of.

Burn circle in the field out back
    past the garden.

Burning, love for, subsequent to
    accidents, great desire to set
    the world on fire for years.

Caliber of firearms.

Camera, lens and shutter speed.

Camera, types of,
    35mm
    digital

fingerprint
miniature
Polaroid
press
stereoscopic.

Casts and replicas, equipment for,
 moulage
 plaster
 silicone
 thermoplastic
 wax.

Charred material, collection of.

Chloral hydrate as poison.

Cigarette and tumbler. Snub-
nose .38, repeated beatings,
constant lack of light, and
hat. Tropes of the detective
novel.

Cloud formations in the sky remind me of when I was young
and we'd move from state to
state like the weather does.
On vacation. Everything was
liquid then, and better.

Conflation of my life and lies, of
the truth and that which feels
to me true.

Control, importance of, striving
for, beauty in, fallacy of, complete loss of.

Conversation snippets. Cans tied
with string and hung from the
telephone pole.

Crime begins at home: vandalism; minor breaking
and entering; subverting
phones. Pirate broadcasting.
Shoplifting. Setting traps.

Crisco's sister who used to baby-
sit me when I was younger.
Who was raped and stabbed
and raped. Who died. Whose
loss meant a *what* began as a
germ in the body. My ab-
sence at her funeral. Crisco
my friend. I am sorry but I
couldn't take it.

Cry.

Defenses: madness, rage, fiction,
or self-defense. Also, sometimes, innocence.

Density,
 of blood
 of glass
 of light
 of meaning
 of paint
 of snow
 of soil
 of space
 of text.

Did brother have his arms back
then.

Direction of break of glass.

Dispersion, of glass. Of staining.

Distance of firing shot,
   concentrated explosions
   pattern of damage.

Distrust of social function. Of
   prom.

Distrust your client. She will
   mislead you.

Does it glisten under light.

Does it have an equal and opposite reaction.

Does it move at all.

Does it move like blood,
   in crevasses
   in the linoleum seams
   on glass
   on tables
   through snow.

Doll heads bought from hobby
   stores and pushed down into
   grass. Sometimes I come upon
   them on our property when I
   sit down, tired from running
   through the pines.

Dream, dreamer, dreaming.

Dust clouds everywhere obscure
   what they obscure.

Edge,
   of accident starring Liz and
      Jesse
   of meaning
   of precipice
   of road
   of story.

Ejector marks.

Electric shock.

Electron microscope.

Electron radiography.

Electronic life.

Electronic reconstruction of a life.

Electronic tracking,
   of a heart bowing under
      pressure
   of a heartbeat
   of a person through the ice
   of vocal modulations.

Electrons clustered around a
   heart onscreen.

Elegiac light.

Elegies for everyone, but especially our long-gone heroine.

End suggests a means. Some
   cause. Abuse?

Energy dissipation in vehicular
   accidents.

Energy, kinetic and potential.

Erasure, restoration of.

Ethyl alcohol as poison. As
    intoxication.

Evidence,
    collection of
    containers for,
        book
        essay
        glossary
        index
        story
    tracking it back to find the
        cause.

Explosions,
    concentrated
    diffuse
    forever searing meaning in my
        eyes, in the world
    retina scars caused by,
        opportunities for their
            repair.

Extractor marks.

F

Faultline.

Fiction,
    necessity of
    need for
    truth content of
    use of.

Film: an answer—the movie
    Dead Kids 2 that Liz made in
    response to the original *Dead*
    Kids, which takes place at some
    small Midwestern college and
    is dull and old and long. Me on
    film: a steak knife in my hand,
    serrated blade to throat. Did
    this happen or did it not.

Fire, determining origin of.

Firing pin impressions.

Footprints of my brother and me
    in concrete at the farmhouse,
    which now is sold to someone
    else who got rid of (?) the dog
    we left with them.

Frey, James, who exists here only
    as a ghost, a set of tracks lead-
    ing us, misleading us.

G

Glass,
    backward fragmentation of
    radial cracks in
    specific gravity of.

H

Handwriting,
    primary factors in
    systems of.

Heliotropes pivot to find light.

Herring,
    red
    smoked and kind of gross.

How to choose what to hit: sup-
    pose you are going 50 mph on
    a 2-lane road. Here comes a
    car toward you—and now, in
    your own lane, a second car
    passing it. One is filled with
    eyes. And one with salt and
    returnable cans. Two cars are
    racing toward you—you have
    to leave the road. Suppose
    that you had to choose hitting
    one of the following objects.
    Which is the safest one to hit?
        a. a large tree
        b. a bridge abutment
        c. utility pole
        d. a large boulder
        e. your family
        f. guardrail and then the
            frozen lake.

I

Iceblink.

Icelight after. Pulsing buoys on
    the lake. Snowmobilers' head-
    lights in the ditches, pitching
    wildly.

Identify.

Identify with me.

Identify with me: my brother's
    lost his arms. Everyone who
    sees him asks However Did
    That Happen? And me dumb
    with nothing in mouth or
    mind. It's a terrible conun-
    drum if it's true.

Identity,
    causal
    of properties
    of source
    of unreliable witnesses,
        author
        characters
        narrator.

Inks,
    ballpoint pen
    carbon
    dye
    examination of
    extracted from the body
    iron gallotannate in
    left from love
    logwood
    made from squid
    nigrosine
    nutgall
    printing
    stains left behind from
    tattooing with
    this
    types of
    analphabetic
    waiting for.

Index,
    as matrix for reconstructing
    meaning
    as method for classifying
      evidence
    as way back into the world after
      trauma, after fire.

Instead of analyzing evidence.

Iodine as poison.

Is crashlight over snow.

Is crashsound ricocheting
    through the air like radio or
    signals of distress.

Is descending like the last few
    maple keys in the first snow-
    storm of the year. Is out of
    place.

Is in the shape of a halo. Means
    something else though.

Is light through snow as seen
    from underneath as beautiful
    as I could imagine.

Is serious stuff.

Is symbol.

Is this stuff true? What is its truth
    content? What can be verified
    or fact-checked? What can we
    call it if it's false?

Italian Hall Disaster in Calumet,
    Michigan, 1908.

Iteration.

Jerk, meaning maybe author,
    for bullheadedness
    for cleverness
    for confabulation
    for invention
    for pyromania
    for telling too much.

Justice, is there any in this world,
    in this ordered and categoried
    world.

Justification, for form, for form-
    lessness.

Keeping your balance, impor-
    tance of.

Lead.

Lectins.

Lever-action rifles.

Like looking through a keyhole in
    a world with no keys.

Like looking through a keyhole
    into a bathroom with a cast-
    iron tub, a naked body, and
    steam in the air.

Likes to feel the punishment of
   rain pinpricks on scalp, an
   antidote to fire.

Linen.

Lipstick.

Liz and Jesse.

Liz and Jesse as friends.

Liz, as symbol for, as sum or
   projection of, as repository for
   many things.

Liz, as true character or maybe
   not, as does she exist or does
   she not.

Liz, still life under ice, still good-
   looking under years of ice.

Liz, truth content of,
   is there a real person Liz or is
   there not, and if there is, who
   is she, or who was she if she
   was and is no longer, and what
   does (would) she think of this
   if she could be here to read it,
   if she ever existed in any way
   at all outside of sentences and
   long tongs of snow constantly
   descending.

Liz whom I had wanted for a long
   time.

Liz with me, or not; Liz with me
   regardless.

Magic,
   any sufficiently advanced
      technology appears to the
      observer as.

Magnifying glasses used to con-
   centrate sun, to burn my name
   in wood, to give the smolder
   to some bug.

Matches, used in starting fires.

Medulla,
   oblongata
   of hair.

Memory: a blue mixing bowl
   filled with deveined shrimp
   my mother left behind. I am
   five. I eat it all in the sun on
   the picnic table which is made
   of rough wood. I try to relate
   this to my dad, but he says it
   didn't happen. What then do
   I do with it? The impression is
   so vivid like rings of sodium
   light in my mind.

Mercury, as fleet-foot god
   as measurer
   as poison
   as quick-change artist.

Microscopic evidence, value of.

Minicameras. Fake books in
   which I'd keep French-to-
   English dictionaries. Forged

documents. Home-finger-printing kits. These tools I sent away for in the back of issues of *Boys' Life* that I had hoped would bring me wisdom, or at least detective power.

Moody, Rick, "Primary Sources," *see also* fiction; *see also* non-fiction.

Motion pictures. Light on screens is meaning.

My brother's hair is gold like straw and sunshine. Some honey looks like it. Or like being out all day in sun.

My fascination with crime, exhibit A: novels, hard-boiled detective thrillers, mail-order private-dick kits, badges to pass myself as a shamus. The Hardy Boys. Even the composite of Nancy Drew and the dumbassed Bobbsey Twins. Many of these written under assumed names, under alias (Franklin W. Dixon was a woman and more, Carolyn Keene was several people, some male and some not). Ellroy. Chandler. Leonard. Mosley. Shadow figures looming on a wall.

My fascination with crime, exhibit B: my criminal record, my history of violence, love of rebellion in all forms, predilection to burn or blow up things.

My friend Jesse.

My friend Jesse going into the lake in his car with Liz.

My friend Jesse in that great and gleaming beast, just washed in summer when we'd go to Canyon Falls with friends to jump into the evenings.

N

Names, some of which have been changed.

Nitrates in gunshot residues.

No mark.

Nonfiction, *see also* fiction.

Nouns,
keeping straight
problems with.

Nylon,
in textiles
stockings, Liz's, mother's,
future obsession with.

Nylons.

Obliteration of documents.

Organic poisons.

Origin of fires. Firespring: gasoline and glitter, fuselage and fuel. Origin of fires in past loss. Origin of remaining meaning in the world in gaps left behind by those who've left me unexpectedly.

Packaging materials.

Paper-identification methods.

Paper, marks upon.

Perspiration.

Phenolphthalein test.

Phenomenon of deceleration comes into operation when a car has to leave the road and heave its hit into a pole or a row of shrubbery or a picked-out blackberry patch, a picket fence with tiny doll heads on pikes epoxied onto the points. Your father died today, you tell the stewardess on the plane to elicit sympathy, peanuts, cheap brandy, gum, and kisses. Since then your dreams have been broken glasses, slivers strewn across rug-clad floors. It is safer to be strapped in a plane, inclined up into clouds that coat the fuselage with ice crystals that glitter in the sun. What is a smashup but a scattering of seeds across vinyl seat and open window. The engineers and accident experts familiar with how much difference it makes to decelerate instead of to stop abruptly are nonetheless surprised by how well this works.

Photoflash bulb.

Photographs, distortion in.

Photographs of ice holes clipped from the paper. Everything goes down to the bottom of the lake: Christmas trees after the holiday. Cans. Glass. Cars and bodies. Snowmobiles. Stampsand leftover from processing iron ore.

Pigment, in hair. In paints.

Plagiarism,
    annoyance with
    as appropriation
    as art

as crime
in published stories, novels
in student essays
the punishment for which
    should be maybe burning,
    maybe exaltation.

Playing Billy Idol's "Dancing with
    Myself." Thinking of danc-
    ing to this at drunken prom
    forever.

Pollens.

Predestination.

Predisposition,
    for cheer
    for depression
    for future prison terms
    for high-school dropping out
    for mental illness
    for submersion
    for typing-class breakdown
        flip-out
    for violence
    for wonderful recovery or
        action.

Procedural, police, interest in
    its form and use of form, the
    patterns found in and created
    by it.

Procedures, police,
    applied to memory
    applied to text and recollection
    applied to text for exploration,
        for exploitation.

Questions, of which you have
    many, of which I have many,
    and as such you and I are in
    this case equal to we, to oui, to
    wee—is there anything we can
    say to stand up to the machi-
    nations of the text, or will it
    have its way with us, will it
    knock us to the ground.

Radial cracks in glass.

Radiation.

Rayon.

Red birds in the sky at sunset.
    Or are they bats? And why do
    they wheel like they're going
    to bomb the sun?

Remainders after long division.

Ring.

Ring.

Ring.

Ringing sound of unanswered
    phones, of discarded wedding
    bands.

River delta means spread and
    source.

River means of course the
Mississippi.

River means sturgeon also, means
wading in up to your waist.
Means smelting in the early
morning pre-dawn.

Rock tumbler. Air rifles. X-ray
spex. Cash counterfeiter.
Rocks that hide keys. Magnets
stuck to the bottoms of
cars. FM-wavelength bugs.
Telephone tap kits. Make-
a-Hovercraft kits. Pens that
convert to knives or lights.

Rouge.

Safe,
burglaries
construction of
methods of attacking.

Scene: a car through the guardrail
and through the ice, cordoned
off by police tape and glistening rows of ambulance and
police lights.

Scene: old paper sacks with stacks
of papers. A box of tampons.

Scopolamine.

Seamen, locating, *see also* homo-
phone for, *see also* adolescent
giggle.

Search,
of crime scene
of persons
wall.

Seconal.

Secondary electron radiation.

Secondary evidence.

Secrets,
hidden deeply
never to be revealed
then revealed.

Secretors.

Seizure,
epileptic
of drugs
of evidence.

Self-doubt.

Self-incrimination,
in dreams
in interrogation
on paper
over and over.

Self-portrait as criminal, as killer,
as love, as index.

Sex offenses.

Shipwreck.

Silk.

Skidding distance.

Smoke, around bullet holes.

Smoke, significance in fire investigation.

Spermatozoa.

Styrenes.

Sweat.

Syringe.

Test tubes filled with rust; polished copper fragments; tape with bits of dialogue; floorboard, box of Raisinets.

Thallium as poison.

The female lead: absent curve of shoulder into neck. Absent bit of Liz.

The principles of criminal investigation suggest a how rather than a what. The what is up to us.

The whole hill is riddled through with mines. Quincy Mine has 96 levels. Water has stoppered up the earth to the 6th level, which you can still go in and tour.

This is algebra. A way of understanding.

Though it's warm out now I think of winter. Feel like being kept inside by weather.

Thule, as in ultima, as in apex, true source of North and white forever.

To put my name in char. To tattoo it all on anything with an arm to take it.

Tools and how to use them. This is a story often told by men and taught to men. This is not a critique of that, exactly.

Traffic reports of accident deaths on the radio and in the papers and on the nightly news that comes in two languages often carry the phrase "collided with a fixed object." A large tree, an abutment, an ice gap. A boulder, a stray breakup phrase, a wiretap, a brick house with a telephone line creeping down the back—that is what is meant by "fixed object," and next to a head-on collision it presents the greatest peril to a moving car.

Trails.

Trajectory of any car on any road.

Trajectory of bullet.

Trifle.

Trophy buck heads nailed onto
  wood. Mr. Kurtz. Men's heads
  on pikes. Doll heads just
  bought from stores in bags.

Truth. What is it, what good is it
  to me.

Truth content,
  inscrutability of
  of memory
  of narrative
  usefulness of the term, or not.

Truth serum.

Twist of rifling.

Uncover.

Undercover work.

Urine.

Vehicular accidents,
  instigation of
  investigation of
  types of.

Vice, Brad, *see also* fiction, truth
  content of.

Vinyls.

Volatile solvent, ignition of.

What is a crane called in to pull,
  to winch, to haul out a car
  from an ice scar.

What is a lock of hair in a hand.
  This is the truth right here—
  I clipped a lock of Liz's hair
  after she and Jesse had been
  pulled from the lake. Is this
  sick. It was new. Still in motion. I was on the scene. I
  knew the undertaker. I knew
  there was an answer. Some
  way to possess her sliver,
  some heart, some part of
  her.

What is a microcosm of the whole.

What is a space I am trying to
  limn without entering.

What is a way of saying a thing.
  What is a good reason.

What is all this coming to. What
  is a seed. What is a mint or
  mint leaf.

What is an end to question. What
  is lit. What is unlit. What is
  cut. What is uncut. What can
  be split, and what cannot.

What is an obsession.

What is ankle bracelet. What is
bra and garter, tether, and
extra-sexy dream.

What is apex, apogee. What is an
arc within an arc.

What is burning, what is burned.

What is candlelight (only a little)
between friends.

What is cost. What is a coast, so
far from home, preamble to
the ocean that you've never
seen and never will.

What is done and gone and over.

What is elicited in confession.

What is ex is X.

What is excised, exorcised. What
sometimes gets excited.

What is full of grief.

What is gasoline on stop-sign
light.

What is gloss on lip. What is a
missed invitation for a kiss.

What is hair scent left in a baseball hat.

What is his. Is theirs. Is hers. Is
ours. Is echo and again.

What is if.

What is just a word. Word and
worm. Men and end. Lime

and sparkler light leaving
streaks along my vision for
hours thereafter.

What is k, the coefficient of a
spring.

What is left.

What is less than fire.

What is less than fire is less than
X deserves.

What is light leaked all over
the new water when the ice
recedes.

What is made of fire. What is
burn in air. What is stop
and drop and roll. What is a
telephone reduced to slag in a
blaze. What is an accelerant.

What is magnesium, strips of, lit
in air from below, and turning into blaze, that temporary
glory.

What is motion.

What is motivation. What is
mine. And what is in the
mine.

What is nape of neck. What is
strand of hair. What catches
bits of headlight light as we
pass by cars. What is con-
densation on the inside of
eyeglass glass. What if we
could reach out and touch it,

everything we wanted, right in
front of us.

What is nightlight glistening on
bare skin.

What is not. Is black on white. Is
etch and mark and mar.

What is not so clear. What is
circumspect. What are we
orbiting around.

What is obliterated.

What is oil spread along the
tanned blade of a shoulder.

What is on a stretcher cruising
in the moonlight toward the
emergency room.

What is one winter defined by
barn collapse and 290 accumulated inches of snow.

What is punishment.

What is quiet bounded by snow
as far as the eye, the I, can see.

What is rearview mirror.

What is sawdust, another thing
converted into a tower of
flame.

What is sawdust dropped from
the third-floor stairwell and lit
from the bottom.

What is short but bright and
excellent inferno.

What is terrified eyelid light.

What is the origin of all fires.

What is the outline of an angel
made in snow.

What is this, is hers, is here on
the page.

What is tracks through snowbank
leading to the lake.

What is unanswered.

What is v, a vee, the velocity of
text on page.

What is what always would have
meant.

What is X an anodyne, a coin.

What is yours as much as mine.

What yes would have meant to
me.

What zzz, the sound of comic
sleep, no dreams, means.

Why is it that I need to know.

Why this is important.

Writing,
    age of
    importance of
    order of
    scent of
    veracity of.

X

X-axis,
    as baseline
    reflection about.

X-ray diffraction.

Y

You can't burn things underwater.

You see. Or not. And either way
    you are soon to be released.

You'd think the mines that go
    all throughout the hill would
    weaken it.

You'd think this is an opportunity
    for forgiveness, for metaboliz-
    ing grief and the urge to burn,
    but urge always remains, is
    left behind like stain, like ash
    mark on a forehead, lipstick
    on a letter, the mineral signa-
    ture on the sauna bench or in
    the water cup after the water
    is gone.

Z

Z, letter, as the logical end, as, in
    its own way:

Zenith.

FRAGMENTS: ON DENTISTRY

I live in serious, constant fear of the failure of teeth. My teeth, mostly, though the possibility of others' dental failure also simultaneously fascinates and repels me. Of course this is even more difficult when confronted by the masses of television commercials featuring gleam-toothed young people, their straight teeth propped up like blinding picket fences keeping me just outside their yard.

—

All the time I dream about smashing my teeth—maybe being *curbed,* like in *American History X,* which involves a curb, your jaw, and a kick or stomp from behind—or some other collision between my teeth and something harder than they are. Third-person, I watch my teeth ground down to dust or smashed away.

—

More often, I have dreams of my teeth shattering not under external force, but in a fall, whether through impact with the floor or a stair or the bookcase. This is probably a symbol of something, but I don't know what.

I can see them splintering out of my mouth to fragments on the ground. Do I pick them up or leave them be?

—

Are teeth hard or are they soft? They feel hard—they work to crush many things put directly into our mouths. They chew through jerky, chop ice, which otherwise seems hard, break through rock candy and peanut brittle, gobstoppers, jawbreakers, a thousand pounds of gum. We are shocked when we go to the dentist to be told that we have cavities (tooth decay, technically called *dental caries*). How could these things—our very own pulverizers—develop pits and ruts? According to the Centers for

Disease Control, 84 percent of U.S. children, 96 percent of U.S. adults, and 99.5 percent of Americans 65 years and older have experienced tooth decay. These seem like low numbers from my experience, but okay. They are at least statistics, hard numbers—nonmalleable, incorrigible, safe from assault or erosion. This in spite of a huge amount of cash thrown at dental care in the form of toothpastes, complicated orthodontics, and toothbrushes with space-age names like the Sonicare 6000.

⬦

I have relied on my teeth, have taken them for granted. I mash popcorn kernels with my molars as I watch the television. I flash them at my animals to indicate aggression. Their presence is comforting on Thanksgiving when confronted with the scads of food that my wife's (Midwestern, if that helps) family traditionally serves up. Most of the food is soft, but still requires mastication to go down. The problem with her family is that after we eat Thanksgiving dinner (usually at two or three in the afternoon), a completely different meal is served at six, being an actual supper (as opposed to dinner, which was earlier), consisting of entirely new dishes. This is needlessly ridiculous. But still I enjoy—am even consumed by—this consumption. And my teeth are there to aid me, there to smash whatever down to paste and down my throat into the digestive mechanics of the body.

⬦

A quick capsule history of toothpaste: ashes from burnt mice heads, rabbit heads, wolf heads, ox heels, and goat feet were thought to benefit the gums in AD 23–79. The oldest toothpaste formula—discovered recently, and interestingly proving to be far more effective than eighteenth-century formulae—comes from the ancient Egyptians, and included rock salt, mint, dried iris flower, and pepper. In the eighteenth-century, the formula contained burnt bread. In the nineteenth-century, think charcoal, think powder. Fluoride enters the picture in the 1940s. And now of course it's all chemical and cosmetic to make teeth impermeable, whiter and brighter.

⬦

I watch a lot of hockey, which does not help the dreams. Famously gap-toothed, most NHL players won't even wear face masks or cages. I simultaneously fear and admire them with their gappy smiles and mullets. Pucks are hard. Slap shots are fast. The body bruises, heals, but not the teeth, not really. They only wear protection after they've suffered pucks or sticks or other major trauma to the mouth.

I think it has to do with masculinity.

Or a response to our soft, safe, indoor, antibacterial lives.

This is probably why I watch it.

I wonder why the teeth do not heal themselves, unlike the rest of the body's carnival sideshow.

An article in the October 1978 issue of *Prevention* addresses this question. Short answer: they do, though only on a relatively small scale. It includes an interview with Robert O. Nara, DDS, a self-proclaimed "renegade dentist" from my hometown in Upper Michigan. His position is that good dental care (prevention) can remove the necessity of professional repair, and since the profession makes its money almost exclusively from repair, you can see why he thinks of himself as a renegade.

I never went to him when I was young.

I want to know if he is still alive.

Perhaps I have an alternate life as an experimental dentist. I am intrigued by diseases of the mouth and gums. (I own several books on the topic, more for the horrifying illustrations—like something sampled directly from my dreams—than anything else.)

In truth, though, teeth are soft. My front two top teeth have been worn away over years of I-am-not-sure-what. My dentist in high school thought I was bulimic because of this wear. Perhaps it is due to excessive intestinal gas or acid reflux (though I distrust this designation, this diagnosis, since I see commercials for it all the time, which is in itself suspicious). Or my teeth have worn away because I consumed Coca-Cola in excess in high school. I drank a six-pack a day (by my estimation).

◆

Sometimes we bite off more than we can chew.

◆

In 1945, the year that my father was born, Grand Rapids, Michigan, the city in which I now reside, was the first city worldwide to fluoridate its water. The fluoridation was so successful in reducing dental caries that the control city, Muskegon, Michigan, demanded that their water be fluoridated too.

Flashback: the story starts in 1909 in Colorado, really (though fluoride research began in 1901), with Frederick McCay, a young dental-school graduate, when he noticed brown-stained teeth in the people of one town (called thereafter Colorado Brown Stain, and termed eventually *fluorosis*). This led—skipping ahead—to the identification of water-borne fluoride as the element that caused this brown stain (and in somewhat lower levels helped to prevent tooth decay). So Grand Rapids, a sometimes forward-thinking city in Michigan, a sometimes forward-thinking state, thought about adopting fluoride in its water. Michigan is proud of its ten-cent deposit on bottled carbonated beverages (these drinks are the enemy of teeth; the sugar and acid mean corrosion): it's still the benefactor of kids at hockey games who troll through trash to trade their recovered and returnable cans in for ice-cream sandwiches at the concession, leading thereafter to necessary visits to the dentist (if not through hockey or through carbonated drinks, then through these sandwiches we are eventually delivered to the hands of dentists.) Grand Rapids put into motion and co-sponsored a study of almost 30,000 schoolchildren. This study showed a strong connection between fluoride addition to the water and the decreasing dental troubles of these kids.

Fluoride additions to drinking water have come under a good deal of fire over the last half century. Aside from the wilder theories about the calming slash pacifying effect on the people (fluoride as conspiracy,

Commie plot, etc.), the main debate centers around what fluoride's actual benefits are, and what it takes to get them. (For years, the thinking was that ingesting the fluoride was necessary, though it seems that
simple topical application, *e.g.,* toothbrushing, will do the trick.) So the
debate is whether cities should be forcing fluoride on all users of their
drinking water, or if this is a waste of money, or worse, a public hazard.
Both sides of this debate claim to have medical fact behind them and
impugn the opposition's studies as being medically irrelevant, or incon-
clusive, or biased due to their association with industry.

It is strange that this debate is still ongoing, but there is evidently a
lot at stake.

More than 61 percent of the population in the United States currently
drink fluoridated water.

In the mouth, food is broken down into bites, crushed into a paste, so it
can be massaged down the esophagus and into all that gastric action.

Analogy, maybe: the mouth is to food as the mind is to language.

I avoid rednecks, or at least the ones you see on TV. *Deliverance* had a
hold on me before I moved to the South. (I was under the impression
that I might be enslaved by backwoods hillbillies at any time if I drove
the back roads of Lower Alabama, as they call it there, which means—
I think—Alabama south of Birmingham.) And I'm not the only one;
witness the popularity of the book and the movie and the throngs of
seventies and eighties horror movies in which city folks get off the in-
terstates and outside their easily managed office lives, etc. It is almost as
if since A, we fear the country, and B, the easy symbol for *country* is the
toothless grin, then we fear a total lack of dental care. (Even as we fear
dental care itself.)

I fear TV British people, too. And Martin Amis, yes, before his famous
dental work. But now that he is civilized, is made for TV, well, that's a
different story.

I was not captured or enslaved. I live free and think of dentistry.

•

There is the gum named *Trident*. Meaning *three-tooth* (think Poseidon, Neptune, with that fork), even with my half-assed Latin know-how (there are wide gaps in my expertise, as instead of Latin, I took Ancient Greek—σπραγμοσ, to rend limb from limb, dismember; με μενετε, ο βοεσ, αλλα σπευδετε: don't wait, oxen, but hurry). Who named this gum that claims four out of five dentists recommend it for your teeth?

Flawed marketing now embedded in the culture, in the language.

•

Other Grand Rapids firsts: the country's first hydroelectric plant, the first scheduled air service, the first publicly funded art installation (a sculpture ostensibly *about* motion, "La Grande Vitesse," 1965, by Alexander Calder, the form of which is strangely toothlike).

•

Form connotes and carries with it expectation.

•

Recently, while on a campus visit for a job I didn't get, I was trading adolescent teeth stories with the resident poet. The same dental slash surgical procedure was recommended in the eighties or early nineties for each of us. We had turned it down and felt grateful for this later.

I have a cross-bite (part overbite and part underbite), and my dentist and orthodontist had wanted to break my jaw and reset it so that everything lined up just right. This was to avoid possible future TMJ (temporomandibular [jaw]-joint) diseases slash disorders. Go to TMJ.org (the TMJ association; their slogan: "Changing the face of TMJ") if you want to know more. There was talk that I might develop lockjaw at some point in my life, which always seemed hilarious to me—perhaps due to association with some book I was reading or some Looney Tunes fever dream.

Everything must always line up.

I forget the name of the procedure, but it required a general anesthetic, and as such it carried the risk—it even said so on the form—of death. This was enough to dissuade me from this surgery, and also I would have had my jaw wired shut for six weeks, and this was unacceptable at the time (I was going into my first year at the college I was just transferring to. I was in choir, for God's sake. I had my pride). This must have been a fashionable surgery at the time, as I've run into many others for whom it was recommended (some who had it done, and who are now Beautiful People, I imagine, fit for the lights, the television, or something even better). And while I'm glad I didn't have it done, still what might this procedure have done to halt the natural decomposition of my teeth?

And, besides, everything naturally decomposes, erodes away from what it was, its original form. When we only lived until forty, if we were lucky, this was less of a problem.

Sometimes we wander, wonder.

Sometimes all we are left with is cavity.

A good friend of mine somehow chipped a front tooth on a (soft) pastry. I lost part of a back tooth on a supercrispy waffle fry from the Southern, God-fearing (closed on Sundays) fast-food chain Chick-fil-A. As I am an American, I thought about suing them over this, but as I am a reasonable person, I did not. Dear Chick-fil-A Management, consider this a warning shot across your bow. I could have been on TV, on Judge Judy or the evening news, my tooth nubs sort of gleaming in the artificial light as I sneered my sneer your way.

There is the image of my uncle with his false teeth in a jar at night. Effervescent cleaning action all around.

My wife's family spent $20,000—give or take—on her orthodontic work when she was young. Which is a lot without insurance. As a result she's got good teeth (seven years without a visit, and her mouth was flaw-less, so the dentist tried to sell her on the artificial whitening, which she turned down). This desire for the best, straightened teeth and jaw (the orthodontist also pushed the breaking-jaw surgery on her, which was refused) coincided with her parents' desire and their entrance into the suburban life around Minneapolis (moving from the tiny towns and farms in Minnesota to the city, taking on the city's norms).

Is our desire to tame the mouth like our desire to tame the land into concrete and subdivision?

Who knows what could be growing out slash in there?

It caused her a lot of pain—retainers, braces, relocation and realign-ment of her teeth. She complains now of a slight and occasional ache that the dentist informed her is her teeth moving slowly back to where they started.

In the absence of a controlling hand, everything will find its way back.

Entropy and all.

I had the one good dentist in Tuscaloosa fill the Chick-fil-A tooth (it was just shy of needing a root canal, he told me sternly, without lectur-ing me yet again on my lack of dental health—this being why he was the one good dentist in the city, in my estimation). He put the filling in (I love the word—filling, as it's a filling-in of the hole, the weakest link, the rotted, painful tooth), but said that it wouldn't last forever.

And, as it has been three years, I guess it's about time. Three years is what we mean by not forever now.

According to Sterling V. Mead's 1927 textbook, *Diseases of the Mouth,* a typical examination of the complainant slash patient should consist of the following steps:

1. Complaint.
2. History.
3. Manifestations of Pain.
4. General Oral Examination.

5. Percussion and Palpation.
6. Exploration.
7. Color.
8. Conductivity of Temperature.
9. Transillumination.
10. Radiograms.
11. Pulp testing by electric current.
12. Bacteriological examination.
13. Histopathologic examination.
14. Blood examination.
15. Urinalysis.
16. Serologic test.
17. Differential diagnosis.
18. Treatment recommended.

My dental visits have been somewhat less grandiose. My gums remain. Technology has ostensibly improved.

❧

Of my dental visits, I remember most the *smell* of the drill in my mouth—that scent of bone as it is ground away (it pains me even to write these words) by whatever tool they use. Is it wrong to say *aroma*—is the connotation of that word too positive for this experience?

Do the teeth keep growing after death like the hair, like fingernails? Or, actually, do teeth grow at all? We get new ones periodically (and, rarely, another full set of adult teeth come in for some people in middle age), but do they grow? How strange it is in our evolution, to get two and only two full sets of teeth (why not three? or four?). And if they grow, are they simultaneously worn away so that our grins seem about the same? Or is the progress so slow that it goes unnoticed?

This is one of many equilibriums. I suppose I should say *equilibria* to mollify the Classicists.

❧

There is always something missing from any account of trauma. Sometimes these omissions are accidental.

❧

Odontophobia, also known as *Dental Anxiety,* or *Fear of Dental Procedures,* is the fear of oral surgery, or sometimes—bizarrely—of teeth themselves.

Why is the fear of dentists so much stronger than that of doctors? Is it the natural uneasiness associated with being out of our zone of knowledge? (Although the teeth are ours, do we even know their names? Molars, sure, but how about the others—could you point them out?) Is it that the teeth seem so simple—and in fact, they are so simple in their operation, in their constancy (until they fail, that is)—that it's hard to understand the massive cost and pain involved with any kind of dental or orthodontic work? Is it the complexity of dental plans? Or is it that the teeth aren't like the body, which has emissions and intermissions between its sicknesses? Is it that our nearly worldwide love affair with sugar (brown and granulated, white refined, sanding or baker's sugar, pure cane sugar, cubed, powdered, icing, fructose, glucose, maltose, lactose, corn syrup, the modern superpowered high fructose corn syrup) is the direct opponent of the teeth? Is it the requirement (and thus the marker) of money, privilege—perfect, suprawhite teeth—that indicates we're celebrities or made to live our lives on camera?

Are whitened teeth the equivalent of having a massive, well-groomed, landscaped lawn? They both are meant to signify.

Does the fear come down to the invasiveness of a visit to dentist? My wife suggests that her fear of dentists is akin to her dread of gynecologists.

Or is it that we take our teeth for granted (unlike the body, which seems to require more obvious care—vitamins, nutrition, occasional exercise, ice packs, ibuprofen, a smattering of Band-Aids and creams, and such)? After all, they're only teeth. It's not like they're the slowly clogging, hidden matrix of the heart with its constant threat of sudden death.

Is it all the mechanisms of the dental office? The drill whine, the pain of braces or of opening too wide for so long, the fear of body odor and the bubble gum-flavored fluoride paste?

●

There are so many gaps to fill.

●

Dentist v. doctor: fight.

I think people would pay to see it. A bit of well-deserved schaden-freude.

Maybe that just isn't fair, is sadistic, paranoid of me.

The median salary for dentists in America, 2004: $111,747. The dental hygienist's median salary: $65,092.

Whereas: the median salary for doctors ranges from $150,000 or so (for family practitioners and pediatricians) up to well over $400,000 (for brain surgeons). These numbers are from 2002. Each profession requires a lot of school. For dentists, it takes at least eight years of school beyond high school for the roughly equivalent DMD (Dental Medicine Doctorate) or DDS (Doctor of Dental Surgery) degrees, and beyond this there's often further schooling in their specialty). For doctors, as you know, it's even more.

•

Nancy McCune, a hypnotist, asks: *Is it worth $79.95 to have the Dentist Fear gone from your life?*

•

This same filling, constantly being filled in and refilled in, has been getting looser every day for the last five months. Given that I didn't have dental insurance until very recently, I was putting off the inevitable. Last week at dinner my tooth finally began to sing. As in it found its voice, and that voice was pain. I don't know if it was the ice water or the bread or the tannins from the wine, but something was distinctly, and no longer acceptably, wrong.

I wait until something is causing me immediate and sufficient pain to force me to find a dentist. One of my students also weighed in. In his opinion, you wait until you reach a level of pain so that a visit to the dentist could not increase that pain any further.

So I looked into the visit and found my way there only today. Of course there is, yes, a dread. A fear of arcane terminology and grinding bone. Again there are my dreams. And expensive contraptions made of wire, the gummy molds they make of bites. Of lights and needles and the dentist's ironically iffy breath.

•

Do I brush and do the desperate last-minute flossing thing before I go in there—dental cramming—or do I eat garlic chicken and revel in his (dentists are more often he than she) discomfort? I cling to this illusion of control.

◆

You should floss for the seven days immediately before your visit if you want to successfully fool the dentist into thinking that you floss every-day, my hygienist tells me.

◆

The television is all about the truth. The camera, as they say, does not lie.

Also the television is all about the teeth.

And the teeth are all about the show: rappers getting gold caps or diamonds set in their front teeth. Our teeth say something about us. They are—even in their utter slavery to convention, to conformity—individual. In case of overwhelming burn or explosion, or the crushing of the body, or major defacement, forensic scientists can identify bodies using dental records. Our dental records—X-rays and bite molds and bite splints and the patterns of tartar (also known as *dental calculus,* a mixed deposit of inorganic salts) and decay along our teeth, our gums eroding faster than our hairlines—are idiosyncratic. They brand us, identify us. The Latin root, *ident-,* meaning *same*—plays out in both *identity* and *dentistry.*

See those stacks of numbered, named children's bite molds stacked beside me in my dentist's too-small office? There are about five hundred piled up from the floor, all dating from years ago. Molds are the inverse of teeth, the opposite of our mouths. I'm sure they're here because of a lack of storage, but en masse they are an index to a generation's dental past. A graveyard of former problem mouths. All the dentists I've ever visited must have a dozen molds with my name on them. How long do they hold onto these? Can I ask for or buy mine back? How long do they retain meaning?

◆

I come to the new dentist on the recommendation of a colleague who tells me that Dr. W. will not make me suffer. At least not without purpose. His office is in what used to be a gas station—not the kind with a big convenience store, but the kind with a small area selling a few candy bars and sodas, and then mostly a garage. The waiting room is modified from where the cash register would typically be. The receptionist tells me that the practice will be moving in six months across the street to a new building with better lights and a more technological and reassuring setup.

Several mothers with children sit inside, waiting. An elderly man is on his way out (this perhaps I fear most about growing old—the dental difficulty that accompanies it, orthodontic goodness and what-have-you. Think my uncle with his false teeth again. Think that corrosion of the mind, of minding the gap), and I bump into him. Apologize. He looks at me as if I'm taking my life for granted. Sit down and pick up an old copy of *People*. Isn't there ever worthwhile reading at these places? Not that I am averse to *People* or to people, but everyone knows the magazine is about dreams, not people: all those unmediated straight white grins can be hard to take.

●

As I write this, one of my students turns in an essay on dental visits, and the feeling that he gets that he continually reads the same magazine over and over again in the dentist's office, since they're all out of date and forgettable. His essay is a paean to his dental hygienist. He spins it Kafkaesque, which isn't all that far off base.

●

Dr. W.'s son is just completing a BA in English. He is interested primarily in writing poetry. He will address different gaps than his father does.

●

The world has seen many great old toothpastes since they debuted (first TV ad in 1955, which coincides with the first fluoride toothpaste, Procter & Gamble's *Crest*; the first print ads appeared, obviously, before with the first mass-market toothpaste products—then called primarily dentifrices, typically in the form of powders—in the late 1800s), though you wouldn't know this by visiting your local drugstore, supermarket, megamart. The shelves are now dominated by varieties of Crest, though still Colgate and Aquafresh hang on (plus the somewhat upscale Mentadent, so fashionable a couple years back, and a few sensitive-teeth toothpastes like Sensodyne), and if your store has a really surprising variety, you can still get Gleem, Aim, Close-Up, Pepsodent—classic toothpastes, all.

The ad and brand language of toothpastes is fabulous—all sciency and adjectival: *Icy Blast Whitening, Anticavity Fluoride Gel, Tartar Control, Baking Soda and Peroxide, MaxFresh Fluoride with Mini-Breath Strips, Coffee Drinkers' Whitening, Multicare, Peroxicare, Total Advanced Fresh, Antibacterial Dry Mouth Gentle Mint Gel with Calcium, Sparkle Fun Flavor, Full Protection Maximum Strength, Advance White Brilliant Sparkle, Fresh Impact, Extreme Clean with Micro-Active Foaming Action, Sparkling White Fluoride Toothpaste with Baking Soda and Peroxide Mint Zing, Zooth Paste: Care Bears Anticavity Fluoride Toothpaste Berry Bubble Flavor Gel, Toothpaste Plus Scope Cool Peppermint Liquid Gel, Cinnamon Rush, Fresh Confidence, Sensitivity Protection Maximum, Rejuvenating Effects, Barbie Anticavity Fluoride Toothpaste Bubble Fruit, TheraBreath Fluoridated Tooth Gel with Aloe Vera, Dr. Fresh Dental Travel Kit, Sassy Coolin' Droolin' Teether Birth +* (the only representative from the baby toothpaste market that I am including for its poetry), *Classic Red Gel, Dental White Professional Patented Tooth Whitening System, Simply White Clear Whitening System, Shane Kosher Toothpaste With Aloe Vera, Fibro-Smile, Sparkle with Fluoristat, Dual Action, Citrus Breeze, The Smokers' Whitening Toothpaste* (there is a toothpaste for everyone; we are individuals and require this).

And then there is the litany of mints: *Icy Cool-, Brisk-, Refreshing-, Crisp-, Whitening Cool-, Clean-, Ultra-, Mild Mint Paste, Extreme Herbal, Energizing-, Minty Fresh Striped, Frosty Mint Striped Gel, Refreshing Vanilla Mint, Wintergreen,* and *Classic Spearmint.* My current toothpaste (no joke) is *Aqua-Fresh Extreme Clean: Empowermint.*

It is most definitely righteous. It foams and foams with its semi-scientific "microactive bubbles." The foam is red so you don't notice if your gums are bleeding when you brush them. Sometimes we do not want to know.

Gone and no longer available are toothpastes like *Rubifoam Dentifrice* (1890s), *Brown's Camphorated Saponaceous Dentifrice for the Teeth* (1890s), *Sozodont Dentifrice: Pure and Fragrant!* (1890s), *Darkie!*

(1950s–'70s, featuring a hugely offensive caricature of a black man in a top hat with blinding white teeth, made by Hawley & Hazel Chemical Co. (available overseas in Hong Kong, Indonesia, etc.). A mutated version of *Darkie!* called *Darlie,* now featuring a white man in a top hat with blinding white teeth, is still selling in Hong Kong), *Stripe* (1960s), *Signal* (1960s, still available in Europe), *Starkist* (1930s—yep, made by the canned-tuna folks), *Avon Toofie* (1960–1970s), *WW Wrigley* (1900–1910s), and *Colgate's Ribbon Dental Cream* (1921).

There are several excellent collections of toothpastes in the world, but the largest is owned by Val Kolpakov, a dentist who lives in Saginaw, Michigan. He has well over 800 tubes. See highlights from the collection at <toothpasteworld.com> or in person in Saginaw. His favorite item is a Scotch-whisky flavored toothpaste with "no more than 3 percent alcohol" from the 1960s.

❖

Fracture is a kind of structure.

There are rules about how things break, in which specific ways they can be broken.

Ask any metallurgist or materials engineer.

❖

Celebrities rarely appear in my dreams and never in my dental dreams.

❖

Fillings and radio: you have heard this story (most famously involving Lucille Ball), though it may be an urban legend: people have occasionally been able to pick up radio broadcasts unaided through their metal fillings. While nearly all scientific journals discredit the idea, still reports persist. The ADA gets an inquiry about this every six weeks or so.

❖

The essay lacks teeth, is instead a ruminant, or is instead a cud itself.

❖

Maybe the problem with the dentist is the intimacy of the mouth— something is wrong *inside* the mouth. And not inaccessibly so—it's not like the appendix is going, a part that we never see and rarely think about aside from shows like the enduring *ER* or other medical dramas that bring out our fear (these things are on the rise—witness the great Fox show *House,* NBC's *Scrubs,* and the cancelled *Medical Investigation,* ABC's popular *Grey's Anatomy,* FX's *Saved,* the forensic-oriented shows like *Bones* and the *CSI* diaspora, and the options only get broader on digital cable; clearly we love our diluted and sexed-up, superdramatized and washed-clean science). There's no way to the stomach except through the mouth. The mouth is how we encounter the world, how we process the big blue awful orb, how we chew it up and reduce it to digestible pieces (we use these metaphors for many other things—thus they are basic methods of thinking about the world).

There is something about the basic functions of life like this—eating or drinking without assistance—that defines us as independent, adult, not disabled.

The mouth is our only serious point of intake (aside from some suppositories and the white lines of cocaine laid out on the mirror, the IV, etc.).

◆

Possibly this essay is like a mold stacked up in a dentist's office—space left behind by something harder—an echo of a form. Or the form itself? To put it another way, is this cavity or is this tooth?

◆

It is all about control.

◆

A dentist visit couldn't be less about control. I'm passive as the young hygienist tilts me back in the chair with the movable head rest (slightly smaller than the back of my head, thus creating a sort of uneasy balance) behind me. Everything is made of steel or white. There are some cheery murals on the wall. Oldies play through tiny speakers. This does not make me like the classics any better. Hold still, she says. Open here, she says. I am taking instructions. I am being tended to. Also I am not in charge.

The mouth is the repository of most of the bodily fluids: blood can come out here (as it has with me—the tissue surrounding my loose fill-ing bled over the weekend—and don't we hate it when we floss and the flossing makes us bleed), and there is all of that saliva which must be suctioned out to keep us from having to swallow constantly. Phlegm (such repellent words we choose for these materials—saliva, mucous, phlegm) perhaps finds its way here. No bile or stomach acid except in unusual circumstances.

Maybe I have an oral fixation? I love food and beverages. From grade school through high school I chewed my pencils, pens, rulers, erasers, nails—whatever. It's surprising that I didn't take up smoking, what with my liking of things to chew on, to keep worrying in my mouth. (The not-so-penitent tobacco industry suggests that maybe it's not too late—this essay is brought to you by Aqua Fresh and Virginia Slims if they still exist, what with their Empowermint and all.) Toothpicks are great, except I have a fear of falling with one in my mouth (there's always fear involving the mouth part of my body). There's that shot of Sylvester Stallone from the movie *Cobra* with toothpick and curled lip. Pretty badass. Hope he doesn't trip. This is what stays with me—the shape of his mouth.

Everything is on camera: maybe there will be a new and awful real-ity show (*Fear Factor: Orthodontist*). My friend Heidi informs me that her dentist has a camera and television screen so the patient can follow along with what the dentist is doing inside! The mouth is a private body part—only shared with, at most, one partner at a time (I can't think of an exception to this—we are made to connect orally).

❧

The tooth is a technology. The essay is a technology.

❧

Vagina dentata. Again, teeth, and urban myth. Another fear. Or renegade pseudo-feminist manifesto. According to Googlism.com (a meta-filter—a filter of the filter that obscures the form with another layer, that as-sembles Google results to create the following matrix of meaning):

—vagina dentata is a tragic farce fought out on the twin land-
    scapes of modernity and postmodernity

—vagina dentata is our warm slinky little pet

—vagina dentata is dark and despairing

—vagina dentata is een geliefd onderwerp onder cyberfeminist-
ische kunstenaressen

—vagina dentata is a short and charming scene of power ex-
changes and sentimentality within a sexual relationship

—vagina dentata is the mouth of hell, a terrifying symbol of
woman as the "devil's gateway"

—vagina dentata is great

—vagina dentata is capable of physically killing him

—vagina dentata is a universal archetype

—vagina dentata is programmed to offer pleasure to men

—vagina dentata is joined by a pussy cum dripping panics

—vagina dentata is classic porn videos name free sex teen

—vagina dentata is a vagina with teeth

—

Sometimes fragments align themselves into useful constellations.

Sometimes they simply travel out through space: these trajectories,
this evidence of fracture, shatter, these things that inevitably remain.

SUBJECT TO WAVE ACTION:
A THERE AND A BACK
(WITH ORCHESTRAL ACCOMPANIMENT)

> *SAILORS: For we sail the ocean blue,*
>   *and our saucy ship's a beauty;*
>   *we are sober men and true,*
>   *and attentive to our duty.*

> (This and all italicized quotations are from
> Gilbert and Sullivan's *H.M.S. Pinafore.*)

PART 1: NOTES FROM THE VOYAGE OUT, IN WHICH OUR PROTAGONIST SETS SAIL FOR THE FIRST TIME SINCE HE WAS VERY SMALL AND CONTEMPLATES VARIOUS SORTS OF GAPS AND EMPTINESSES AND FINDS OUT IF HE IS SUSCEPTIBLE TO SEASICKNESS OR NOT AND REALIZES THE POSSIBLE PHYSICAL CONSEQUENCES OF THE USES OF DRAMAMINE

Sea green buoys, lots of floating muck that congregates in blocks: pieces of a puzzle much larger than I can put together. The lake is calm, the sky clean, like a marble counter, like an operating table. Several piers surround the boat with their towers of gravel and huge chunks of broken-up concrete. Seagulls roost atop floating dirty patches, form that tops off formlessness. I am, at this point, afloat in a harbor just off Muskegon on the eastern edge of Lake Michigan—about to be unmoored from the dock and my life on dry land. It's not as if I haven't been on a boat before, but I haven't been on a boat this far away from land, out in the middle of one of the Great Lakes that define this part of the country, and I haven't been on a boat that had decks or different traveling classes, haven't been so far out on the flat chopping board of the lake that land is out of sight, and I can't imagine anything else beyond this beyond. The boat does not care about my fear, about my abdication of control for the next few hours, and I feel a slight drift, and we are moving.

There is talk behind me—this boat, this newer, made-in-Alabama-and-shipped-up-to-Michigan boat (which seats 248 passengers, 46 cars, and 12 motorcycles) is said to be smoother than the older SS *Badger*, which leaves from Ludington and gets into Manitowoc, one of those Native American-named towns that dot the shores of Wisconsin.

Reasons for the circumvention of Chicago: the massive coils of traffic, the constant truth of construction, all implied by the only serious skyline in four hundred miles. Really it is the only *major* traffic problem in the whole middle of the country, snarled and constantly unfurling, Chicago, I-94, I-90, I-80, I-280, I-294, and I-290, plus I-55, I-355, and I-57—every major interstate meets up right at the southwest corner of this lake that I am on, that I will cross in this way.

"What are you knotting there, my man?" "The knot." (Herman Melville, *Benito Cereno*)

Our staff consists of Captain Pollett, first mate Chris, with Katha and somebody else onboard. We hear these things on the intercom system that's piped throughout the interior of the cabin. I sit in the seats reserved for Passengers Accompanying Wheel Chairs. While I am A Passenger Not in a Wheel Chair, there are no wheelchairs onboard so this seems fair.

There is a safety video that they are showing. I cannot see it, but the voices infuse the air. It might be coming from Premier Class, a first class that doesn't seem superior or in any way premier enough to justify its cost (about double the standard fare). It's walled off in a separate room, and they have free drinks and electrical outlets on every table. I stop in to ask one of the attendants why anyone would want to pay double to be in Premier? "No kids," she says and shrugs.

The waves pick up a notch—the remains of gasoline make tracks across the water. There is information to be had: life rafts and life jackets are onboard for 400 persons, though the ship only carries 248. They come in under-90-lbs and over-90-lbs varieties. The fattest among us will probably need two or three. They are stowed in lockers and on the sundeck. We are (the ship is), as we are informed, "subject to wave action" when we are onboard. So we are asked to be careful and refrain from leaning over the railings. The video tells me this beast is 191 feet, 57 feet wide, 46 feet tall (waterline to top of radar mast). It is a twin-hull catamaran, like a giant Jet Ski. "This is definitely not your grandfather's ship," it says eroding into high-tech blah blah.

This is more true for me than it is for some. My grandfather was the captain of several ferries before the construction of the Mackinac Bridge and the official linking of the two peninsulas of Michigan. He ferried cars, cargo, and people across the Straits of Mackinac for years before the bridge. The *Vacationland* was his last ship—this I know or think I know.

The sun is out, and it looks beautiful. I have never been completely surrounded by water, aside from baths and smaller lakes, speedboats, summers spent trying to get up on waterskis and wiping out, accumulating bruises. I am not opposed to water, but it doesn't have the allure for me that I equate with a certain naval and often male fantasy. Two of my high-school and college friends have joined the navy. One is a cryptologist (or cryptographer), or so he tells me. When he was stoned he sometimes spoke cryptically, like a Dungeon Master might, but that's about all I can summon in favor of the theory of his enlisting. My other friend attended the Annapolis Naval Academy and until recently was commanding a battalion of amphibious assault vehicles in Qatar and other exciting places. I would not have guessed either of them to be fit or meant for the sea.

We pass outside the long piers that jut into the lake like exclamation points. I have some trepidation, having never done the cruise-ship thing; I can barely do the relaxing thing or the floating-on-my-back-in-lake-water-with-strange-fish-darting-by-below-me thing. The water is getting slowly choppier. And we come up to lake speed (39 miles an hour on average) in just a second or two—there's the last lighthouse before we hit the wide expanse. And now I can feel the wave action that we are apparently subject to, this rocking motion, this back and forth that we feel going there and back. The rocking is accompanied by a rocking sound track pumping through the speakers—vaguely distorted theme music that's been composed for this experience because our lives must be accompanied by theme music at all times so we know how we should feel about events. Music in this way hovers on the edge of recognition—it's familiar but not quite right, and it slides off the deck and down under a wave.

The boat is new, less than two years old, and everything is mostly clean in that modern way. The walls are flecked, some sort of plasticized particle board, the kind that won't look dirty even if it is (and won't look completely clean, even if it is—which it is not, though it's hard to tell without close examination—scratches and scuffs darken it in constellations).

There aren't that many waves just yet. Lake Michigan gets waves twelve feet and higher sometimes, but nothing like that today. I will be returning on the boat tomorrow night, and rain is forecasted then. One problem with the Lake Express ferry is that it won't go out if waves are expected to be greater than nine feet high, and so occasionally passengers are stranded for a day or an afternoon on one side of the lake or the other.

As the land that looks like a diorama behind us dwindles, we are left with flatness. This expanse is one kind of isolation. It is like living in Iowa if the whole state were underwater (which it probably will be again in the distant geological future). Feels like reading Melville.

A lot of people consume baskets of burgers and fries here on the boat. I had an Enormous Omelet Sandwich from Burger King, my first expedition into this particular gastronomic hell. The boat is a sort of microcosm of American crap, a floating mall, with a large snack bar hawking caesar salads, breakfast frittatas on croissants, Mike's Hard Lemonade; there are televisions everywhere, kiosks selling magazines, CDs, Dramamine—

> As an aside, the lethal dose (LD50) of Dramamine in rats is 500 mg/kg. LD50 means that at this dose, 50% of the subjects die. There is another use for Dramamine, in that taken in larger amounts, it causes tripping with hallucinations—

This corrugated flatness. This constellation of evolving flecks and dips.

If you live close to a Great Lake, you know the song, "The Wreck of the Edmund Fitzgerald." Where I am from in Michigan there is the constancy of ore boats coming through the canal, a reminder of former industrial boom. We regularly wait for one of the largest lift bridges in the world to raise its main section for the thousand-foot boats to pass underneath. Do they have to pay for this convenience, I wonder? We wait in line in traffic, we go to bars and hear acoustic covers of the Gordon Lightfoot song before the inevitable segue to "Hotel California." We have the mining, geology, and maritime museums. Some of our relatives worked on the boats that supported the mining industry and connected the holes in the ground to the rest of the world. Some of our relatives went down in shipwrecks or dive for their bones among the extreme museums of the sunken wrecks that dot Michigan's half of the Lake Superior coast. We live our lives surrounded on at least two sides by water, on the peninsula. The boats—the *Ranger I*, the *Ranger II*, the *Ranger III*—are ways out for us. (The first two have sunk; the third is gonna sink, so goes the unfunny childhood joke.)

But when you're actually on a boat, out on the water, the song means more. We are echoes of our relatives who spent their lives on water. We are subject to wave action, to capsizing or sinking. Seriously, we could die or float forever, devoured by six-foot muskellunge. It's a little scary. You have to reckon with it.

Michigan's a state connected over water to Canada; to Illinois, Indiana; to Wisconsin and to Minnesota.

Space break because it's a whole different story up on the sundeck: I have to admit this is awesome—big wind, great sun. Quite cold since it's maybe fifty degrees without the windchill, and this means I won't be out here for long as my fingers are getting white even as I type this little bit on my titanium Apple Powerbook. Man in a suit and sunglasses looking cool and patriarchal. *I'm on top of the world! &c.* And it's hard not to feel patriarchal—we are on top, in charge, athrust this huge fucking machine. The water blasts loudly out of the twin backs of the boat. Two kids, maybe thirteen each, dressed up in sweatshirts and jackets, are rolling a golf ball between them on the deck. They're laughing, especially when the golf ball bounds over the edge, ricocheting down the hull into the lake. Major water hazard. You have to take a drop with a penalty I tell them. They laugh, think I am a dork, and leave, and then I am alone. I am hardy enough to be the sole witness to this spectacle for the moment.

It does make me want to find Jon Krakauer or join the navy, especially if I get an outfit.

I walk around the back. One of the Lake Express employees adds some reflective red tape underneath the door to the Premier Class cabin—possibly someone fell here, or has thought of falling, and has thought of suing. Her job, she tells me, or I dream she tells me, is to go around the ship and think like a passenger. She is a tester. She is supposed to be dumb, to anticipate others' stupidities.

Is there any reason I can't just go back through the Premier Cabin into the interior? The safety video told me not to do it, that it was prohibited, but I can't see why. It is the most direct route.

It is more pleasant on the lower outside deck, at least as far as wind goes—this is doable, I think, for an hour or so. You get the same sun, but you can only see where you have been. This view is a view of the past—the twin wakes, the smell of gasoline, a few Premier Class sorts sunning on the back. They look about as Premier as you'd expect. They have no kids. One of them seems drunk.

Now we're getting a more pronounced rocking motion. Cigarette stink and there I see my coffee-cup cozy that I lost in the wind and blaze up top. It flops down to the deck and sits there. The question is, do I pick it up? No, I do not. A man in a windbreaker, khakis, and Birkenstocks stands astride it right now. If I were to reach between his legs to grab it, that might be seen as somehow untoward. Even though we are at sea, in a way, there are rules of conduct. Especially at sea, what with the intricacies of maritime law. Those kids run by again with another golf ball in their hands. Did they bring a package of range balls with them for this purpose? It's hard not to be like them, not to want to throw shit off the sides: bottles with or without messages, golf balls, coffee cups, my coffee-cup cozy, fishing lures, this laptop (and free myself from this technological life forever), or whatever.

It's true that I have put messages in bottles and thrown them in the water farther north where I am from. I once found a bottle in the water with a phone number inside. I called that phone number and received no answer maybe sixty times before giving up months later. Eventually I lost it, no longer kept it with me, no longer thought of its importance. This was before my phone-phreak days, days of concerted technological competence; at that time I did not know how to get the physical address, the number's referent, what it represented, the body behind the phone line. These numbers, ethereal things without resolution, connection to the outside world: they have multiplied—they now surround us. Much of the world is hidden behind scrims of unlisted numbers, prepaid cell phones, the apparent magic of IP addresses, domain names directing us through proxies, prows to other countries and back, web sites erected and gleaming in the sun. If I knew enough, I could track these redirections back to flesh.

I wanted to get in touch with whoever put their number in that bottle and threw it in the water. I might have found it years later—decades later as the bottle floated in from the Atlantic Ocean through the Soo Locks and all the way. Maybe my parents threw it in the water a few minutes before to bless my brother and me with mystery, with a mystery that lasted—at least for me—for years. Even now I remember this interaction with the Other.

Or, reaching further, it could have been my grandfather ferrying boats across the Straits who dropped it years before, in a romantic or melancholy moment, and through the chaos action of the water it found its way somehow to me. I like to think of it that way, or as a threat of romance— an unknown beautiful girl reaching out toward another apparition somewhere in the future, or perhaps the past.

There is the head, and then there is the water—the complete expanse of it—which suggests the infinite. The land behind us is, I think, gone— I see a haze but nothing's really there: it is an optical illusion since we are about halfway across right now. Nothing is on any side of me. All there is *is* and water, some horizon, blue forever. Water as backdrop to the action on the boat, to the action of the boat against or on top of the water, displacing it, sucking it in and blasting it back out into wake, doing who knows what to terrify the fish.

A thumbnail-sized fleck of gray paint falls down from the top deck— all that wind's action on it. Erosion always happening above me, all around me.

Contemplation—

> and I am dazed

> amidst this space.

I guess I don't get seasick—at least not lakesick on this big-ass lake. I am getting weirdly hungry though. How does one get the job of piloting the boat from shore to shore? Aside from the necessary loneliness, it seems good to me.

I drink my grape Propel Fitness Water made by Gatorade (garnished with Splenda, the latest advance in artificial-sweetener technology), which is sort of refreshing in the chemical way you would expect. I sip my drink and contemplate the infinite exteriority of the world.

Shortly afterward I have to pee, which shuts my thinking up. I contemplate peeing directly into the lake, but of course I won't—that would be indecorous—hardly befitting a man of my sudden honorary naval stature. I want to try my cell phone, see how far away we are from service. I go into the Premier Class cabin, directly through and to the bathroom, and am not bounced or seen as an impostor.

The bathroom is as you would expect, like a plane's but bigger, with less anxiety. Everything's still encased in this grayish particle board with constellations of multicolored flecks. In the bathroom it's mostly clean, or as clean as it can reasonably be. There are panels all around. You can hear the boat as it gives and moves.

I am back on the sundeck, which is where I'd prefer to be for the whole trip except for the constant battery of wind. It's easier to be atop the boat than to be stuck inside it. The boat appears to slow, though it could be just a cessation of the wind and the resulting quiet. I can hear the radar widget rasp above me as it revolves.

> BUTTERCUP: I've treacle and toffee, I've tea and I've coffee,
>   Soft tommy and succulent chops;
> I've chickens and conies, and pretty polonies,
>   And excellent peppermint drops.

A fifty-year-old woman in old-people wraparound sunglasses smokes intently on the back deck with me. I have been onboard an hour and a half. Another woman has a huge thousand-page book on her lap, and she dozes in the sun. Her husband returns from the land of Snack and deposits a packet of peanut M&Ms on her lap. I witness some appreciation. This two and a half hour ride is one of the few moments of unbroken leisure I have had in the last month, though even now I am examining it, trying to whip it into whatever shape it will take. I can see the attraction of the cruise-ship situation.

I am surrounded by men contemplating something larger than themselves—six of them stand along the aft end of the ship gazing out, legs spread shoulder-wide or more in a form of dominance, maybe, or just for stability, staring at our wake. Are they admiring its bigness, the complexity and sheer size of the world, or are they thinking about whether they have to piss in it, what responsibilities they have back home, or on the other side, in Milwaukee? Is it easy to forget the land in just a couple hours? Or is it like the sea lore and songs, this song I sang in high-school choir, "Song of the Sea," which I sang at some point at an open mic in college (I'm not sure why, am no longer sure why I did the majority of the things I did in college—this past a country receding quickly out of sight), and my friend, who had a big crush on me, told me it was beautiful. Was it really beautiful or was it not?

I think of *H.M.S. Pinafore*, in which I played a role in high school. I think of the dominance of maritime life before the advent of flight, the predominance of boats and ships in emigration and immigration, the idea and etymological root of *shipping*.

Land ho! some kid yells up on top. Milwaukee has been sighted. I consume a celebratory M&M. Evidently kids still read or watch things on TV about sailing and/or pirates. I will, I think, conclude by staying up on top and watching land approach again.

Standing on the top deck, I can't avoid Gilbert and Sullivan—it's great; the songs resonate with me anew. I was a sailor. We had to sing and dance a jig. There may have been pantaloons. I was not well-suited to the stage.

The buildings of Milwaukee and the coast of Wisconsin appear now out of the haze. The only good place to stand on the top deck and be out of the wind is behind a small tower spiked with antennas. I stand there until I see the "bathroom exhaust fan" grate right in front of me.

Now it is all men on deck. There are five of them standing and facing into the wind as we approach landfall; also a mannish woman. What are they (we) trying to recapture, to prove?

We disembark and enter into the city with all of its ruined, industrial beauty. I grab my things and I am out of there.

—

PART 2, IN WHICH I RETURN FROM THE WESTERN SHORE AND BEGIN THE VOYAGE HOME WITH A MUCH STRONGER SENSE OF TREPIDATION GIVEN THE GATHERING CLOUDS AND THE HISTORY OF LITERATURE FEATURING SHIPWRECKS, WHALE ATTACKS, GIANT SQUID, PIRATES, CANNIBALISM, AND THE DWINDLING POSSIBILITY OF SURVIVAL

I look forward to the return trip with less enthusiasm: it will be a nighttime voyage, with less to see, and the possibility of storms.

My friend Victor drops me off from his large black Chevy SUV and comes inside the ferry terminal to use the bathroom. We hug without much awkwardness. We are large and we are men, and we are on land and it is good. As I push through the security checkpoint, Victor turns to go, and then he goes, and then there is only the memory of Victor and the churning crowd and darkness beginning.

The light fades quickly as we exit the Port of Milwaukee. The boat maneuvers itself between the breakers. It is difficult to stay up top because of the wind and especially because of the sheeting rain and the wet metallic deck. I am cornered in a conversation with a guy who wants to talk about skydiving. He is large—his belly expansive as a table—and I find it hard to imagine him skydiving, aside from his obvious enthusiasm for the subject.

Inside I have my porthole, and the sky is fading into blackness. The horizon is two-toned as the light fades and the colors approach one another, unifying. It is 6:30 p.m., and we are on our way back across the endless lake.

On the back deck I can again feel the wind—from inside you can hear the ticks of rain spattering against the double-paned window, and you can see the tracks of water running down the outside glass. You are aware of the idea of wind—that it must rush by outside, but you're insulated from it, from the actual experience of travel. But push through the "Push Hard: EXIT" door and it is another story. I stand at the back of the ship and watch the boat's engines churn the black water into foam, which then slowly settles down into the artificial calm that indicates the track the boat (and then the wake) took recently across the lake. I wonder about the technology of it. No one is outside to witness this minor miracle except for me. It is cold and dark and wet, and it is beautiful now being alone here in the midst of this loneliness that is us—a boat against the surface, a perk in the middle of all the perky and rained-upon water. And because it is dark, it's easy to understand the world as this—as only us along the edges of this boat, some of us inside with $3-rented headsets watching the wretched postmodern remake of *Bewitched* with Will Farrell and Nicole Kidman, and some of us facing outward toward the water. *Anything* could be out there—we could be *anywhere,* unlocated, adrift, in this world of GPS and Google maps.

Of course we are here, somewhere between Milwaukee and Muskegon, and all of us are together, but this is what our lives are right now—all vector and containment, the displacement of thousands of pounds of water and us speeding all alone above it. The remains of one of my grandfather's ships—pick any of them—could be submerged several hundred feet below us in this other, water world. I think that's why I love the water—it conceals, it separates one world from the other, it stands in as metaphor for the subconscious in psychotherapy, in dreams.

All you can see out the window is the dust collected in between the panes, the dust reflecting light, and almost opaque, and even if there is nothing out there to see, I can see our reflection in the glass and through the dust.

It's hazy.

There is a constant motor hum.

There is the creaking of the paneling above me. Children shriek intermittently like animals.

We are all in this together—if we sink, we will all sink. We could be on an episode of *Lost* except that we are colder, fatter, more docile; less diverse, ambitious, and attractive. We could feast on the collected boxes of Bigelow tea and the remaining flavored malt liquors that stock the boat. It turns out that I'm hungry. I ask the two guys who are working the dinner kiosk which sandwich they would recommend—perhaps the gourmet tuna pesto on ciabatta bread? (Are these words real? Do they mean anything in this new and plasticized, manufactured world?) They both recommend the bacon cheeseburger. I tell them that it sounds like a lot of meat. They say, well, you asked us. So I order one. It's good. There are some limp chips that accompany it, and I eat about a third of them. I eat and think, zone out.

Do I think of my mother? My grandfather? And everyone else who has died before me? Yes, I do. The dark and this individual aloneness bring these thoughts on. This is my infinity, Michigan's version of infinity, of reach and expanse. This state holds this one experience aside from winter: you will eventually lose yourself in or to the lakes (and winter with all its snow is a colder analogue). I suppose Iowa holds the vastness of corn and pervasive pig stink, and Gary, Indiana, holds the vastness of the factories and tiny little houses placed on grids and train lines going nowhere, or going everywhere. And the West has its mountains and the ocean; the Southwest, its desert and occasional casinos. And everywhere has the sameness of the dark or of the nearly constant rain that feels as if it will never stop. But Michigan, my Michigan, has this, this lake, my lake Michigan, though we share custody with Illinois and Indiana, all those *I*s, those eyes watching us from across the lake.

We have a problem of simple definition—you can't make anything out in the dark. Anything could appear before us and be run up against, upon.

I need a brace of wind, so I go out back at first. Skydiving man is out and talking about his travels in the Arctic Ocean. I'm jealous of this emblem of traditional masculinity—I'd love to go that far north. I'd love to have it in me to undertake that sort of travel, that adventure, that Magellan, that Admiral Cook, that Conrad, that Melville thing. But I do not, at least not right now. I push by him on my way up the stairs to the top. The steps are slippery, with water pooling off the traction strips. It is cold as shit, and no one else is here. Rain moves against my face with the help of wind, and it is nearly painful. No, in fact, it hurts. It does. There's a glow ahead of us somewhere—whether it is Muskegon or the lit-up edge of the newly burning world, I can't tell. I can barely hold my face against the wind to look at it. I can only hold the gaze for half a second or so. And the wind and rain just then pick up significantly. I try to get back to the stairs and am blown part of the way before I hook my hand around the railing and trudge back down the dripping, draining stairs.

An hour later there is more definition in the lights that frame the coast. I stand alone up top, as the rain is taking a ten-minute break from its harassment of my eyes and cheeks, and face forward toward Michigan's west coast. Lights spread mostly south, but some north too, all ahead of us. There is another, other coast ahead of us; there is an end to our short voyage. On the starboard side of the boat I can see a huge boat—this one bigger than us, I'd guess, though it's too far out to tell—several miles away. We are alone but not. We have a twin, a secret sharer, something passing by us in the emptiness. And on the starboard side toward the bow of our boat, a high-powered lamp lights up the water and the hull of our catamaran slicing through it. We are moving fast. There is no other word than exhilarating, with a bit of punishment involved. *Fucking A* is what I say—out loud—to no one, at least not to anyone on the boat or in the sea. The water's dark around us. If I were to lean forward and fall across the rail, I would be gone and into the swirl of the lake before anyone could tell. The water's cold, I'm sure, cold enough to kill me after a few minutes of exposure. Imagine being on an icebreaker working through the Straits, completely alone as the ice shimmers and cracks around you. I am looking forward. I feel closer than ever to my grandfather who died before I was born. This is what it must have been like for him. With less wind, since his boat no doubt moved more slowly. This is how I feel at 2 a.m. when no one is on the streets. This is how I imagine truckers feel—*away* and alone, unattached, in transit, privy to this moment, wanting nothing more.

Coda: again, aloneness. I hear the engines being killed, and everyone's excited to be here, to be here for this moment, coming in. About six men get up—almost in one motion—and head up top. There is something to this gender thing, I think, but then there are three teenage girls on the deck singing together—it's like the departure-theme song I heard before, but somehow reconfigured; it's as if they have been practicing for the last three hours and only now have they come onstage for their curtain call. It's dark and we drift through the breakers. There are a handful of flashing lights (green for port, red for starboard). These are indications we are getting there. I'm not prepared for the quiet. With the wind's cessation, and the gap left from the engines cutting out, the boat just drifts. I've read about this before in books: how quiet it is with the boat just drifting under its own power, and now those words feel real to me in a way they never have before. Downstairs you know that the door opens when you hear scattered bits of conversation and squealing kids, snacks being efficiently vended, change being made, the spines of books being cracked open and closed, the world working as it does—gears within gears within gears. And so I go back down and into it again.

> BOATSWAIN: *Well, Dick, we wouldn't go for to hurt any fellow-creature's feelings, but you can't expect a chap with such a name as Dick Deadeye to be a popular character—now can you?*
>
> DICK. *No.*
>
> BOATSWAIN. *It's asking too much, ain't it?*
>
> DICK. *It is. From such a face and form as mine the noblest sentiments sound like the black utterances of a depraved imagination. It is human nature—I am resigned.*

THE LONG CRUSH

First, people, please: it's *disc golf,* not *Frisbee golf.* If you've heard of the sport at all, which is unlikely unless 1) you watch a lot of ESPN2 late at night between Magic: The Gathering tournaments, the National Paintball Finals, and celebrity poker tours, 2) you smoke a lot of pot, 3) you play ultimate Frisbee, which often has a strong correlation with #2 and #4, or 4) you go to college somewhere other than the East Coast. *Frisbee* is a brand of recreational flying disc made by Wham-O, usually 135 grams (which is light, as opposed to a 165-gram ultimate Frisbee disc), whereas disc golf is played with heavier *golf discs* (Wham-O does make a few golf discs, among them the #86 Softie, a classic putter recently brought back into circulation, but their models aren't particularly good or popular). A version of disc golf is called *frolf,* featured on an episode of *Seinfeld,* but that's different as it is played not on dedicated courses but in parks and cities with regular Frisbees. A Frisbee can leave a bruise. A golf disc could probably—though I didn't take enough physics in school to prove it—kill you.

I have spent thousands of hours playing the game on over a hundred courses from San Diego to Tuscaloosa to Canton, where the Pro Football Hall of Fame resides just outside of Cleveland. Mostly in summertime, which is the height of my obsession with the glorious game, between the work of refinishing the floors of my hundred-year-old house and the occasional teaching and catching up on reading during the long breath between semesters. The real test of the devotee, though, is when the summer gives way to cold and fall and leaves start descending, sparkling to the ground. My rule is that I will play year-round if it is above zero, and occasionally I play when it's below. Snow is no real obstacle, though it requires heavy boots and bundling up. Sometimes parks close (disc golf is primarily played in public parks on actual, designed courses with real chain-link baskets, but into which wander kids and dogs, punks and drunks), and I have to circumvent the gates. I've played with guys who tie streamers to the backs of their discs to aid in locating them when they get buried in the banks, beneath the latest snowfall. I have been known to play in rain, in massive windstorms (this is less than fun but good for later narrative), in sleet and hail and drunkenness, in squalls and in tornado weather outside Ames, Iowa, when the sky turns green. When there are sirens and everything is suddenly and suspiciously still, I can get one more hole in before calling it a day and running to a shelter. If a disc were thrown in a tornado, it could potentially travel for miles, maybe forever. The flight could far surpass the flat-land-distance record for a golf disc, currently around 250 meters, set by Swedish golfer Christian Sandstrom—this is an impressive record as the average player can throw about 100 meters. Distance is one thing I do very well, which contributes to my obsession with the game, which is to say I can *crush the disc*—I can throw it 150+ meters on a good day. I am three-eighths Swedish, which may or may not help.

I spend a lot of time trying to convince people that it is (I am) not ridiculous. Or that it's no more ridiculous than any other game or sport. So how can I convince you? It's not as if this game is any more bizarre than "ball golf" (as disc people call it): throwing a disc is a far more natural motion than hitting a tiny dimpled technologically enhanced surlyn- or balata-covered ball with a graphite-shafted Big Bertha stick. I mean, discs are in the fucking Olympics (well, discus, anyhow). That means it's like old and Greek, like democracy and pederasty, unlike ball golf, which hails from Scotland, the land of haggis and the band Del Amitri. It takes much less time—I get in eighteen holes in about an hour if I'm playing by myself, or an hour and a half if I am having more fun with friends. Compare to the four plus hours of your life you'll blow on the ball course. It's far better for the environment (the royal ball golf course in the country of Dubai uses one-third of the country's yearly water supply for upkeep, as an extreme example—compare that to a public park, unwatered, ungroomed, no carts or fertilizer required). It's cheaper (free most places—occasionally you have to pay the public-park fee or a greens fee of $5 or so). And the equipment—in spite of being doubly as cool as ball golf, more on this in a bit—is much cheaper. One disc (six to eight bucks) is all you need to play. You could even play with a regular Frisbee, though I do not recommend that unless you mean to look like a chump. Compare, again, to perimeter-weighted, titanium-headed, graphite-shafted asshole sticks and the gas or electric carts that golfers, especially Southerners, use. And in spite of this I *like* ball golf in all of its bizarreness and history; I own a set of clubs and upgrade them relatively often (always we require our new technologies, our upgrades, our big and bigger toys). I yearn for Ping, for Calloway, for the budget and the skill set of the pros. I play a few times a year with friends or when my in-laws visit. I even enjoy watching ball golf on TV and playing Tiger Woods Golf on Xbox with my friend Neil, a crime writer. Trust me, though: disc is better.

Disc golf lets me indulge in my most geekish tendencies: hoarding (or, if you prefer, exhaustively collecting), a sometimes ferocious competitive streak, a serious interest in the bizarre or esoteric, a liking for diversions of all sorts, a desire for control over the world.

I have been the mockery of my wife and friends, and even my family when they are feeling uncharitable. My car's trunk is filled with discs, and disc-golf bags, disc markers, bug spray, calamine lotion, disc-golf magazines, the international-course directory, and a variety of gloves (I wear a throwing glove to protect my hand and to improve my grip, and to make me seem hardcore, plus there are cold-weather gloves with Thinsulate for inclement weather and the big snowmobile gloves that I wear as an outer shell to keep them warm and flexible when playing in the snow), and did I say hundreds of discs? There are only two major disc manufacturers. Innova (based in the awesomely named Rancho Cucamonga, California, and maker of discs mostly named after animals: Shark, Jaguar, Puma, Viper, Eagle, Cobra, in addition to the more fantastic Archangel, Banshee, Dragon, Orc, and Roc, and the more abstract Beast and Monster) makes most of the discs that I like the best, maybe because of my predilection for strange fauna, my ownership of several *Dungeons & Dragons Monster Manuals,* and the fact that I once attended Gen Con, the big yearly D&D convention, in Milwaukee, with my dad who was kind enough to indulge my obsession. Discraft discs are made in Walled Lake, Michigan, which means I should be loyal to my home state, though in this one case I am not; they make more technologically named discs like the XL and the MRX, the pro-plastic XS, the special modified Z-plastic Buzz, the Flash and Crush, or the more meteorological and menacing—Cyclone, Storm, Typhoon. You can buy a light disc as a starter for your kid, or discs for your dogs, mini-discs to throw inside the house or office, and even tiny baskets to use as targets. Discs come in a variety of weights (from 135 up to 200 grams each, and heavier discs are generally preferred by the more experienced players because of their performance in the wind) and colors, different kinds of plastics, and different molds (some are made for distance, some are designed for the equivalent of chip or midrange shots, for stability in wind, or to turn either left or right when thrown correctly, and others are for putting only, or roller shots, or hammer throws, turnovers, helixes, or forehand drives). And variety is the key, as they all perform differently, so this ensures I'll add more booty monthly to my plastic hoard, my flattish circular menagerie.

I have two hundred discs (give or take a few—and the water and the trees, the concrete and the backs of pickup trucks driving by, they give and take all the time), only about a third of which are seriously in rotation. I carry eighteen in my bag at any given time (yes, I do have an official disc-golf bag after years of carrying around modified purses gleaned from runs to the Salvation Army; these purses have also exposed me to mockery in this more-male-than-not sporting world). I have duplicates in case of loss during friendly play or tournaments. Some of them have been retired after hitting trees (they become less reliable, their flight characteristics changing, with each obstacle hit), and I've kept several discs that have split in half due to hitting trees during subzero play. My policy is to keep the broken ones that have some sentimental value, such as those I've used to hit holes in one—and, in case you're interested, the official PDGA rule is that if a disc breaks in flight you must play your next shot from the location of the largest remaining piece. And some of my discs are for show only, like my limited-edition Starfire, my old Super Roc, and my 2004 and 2005 Championship Rocs (the most valuable disc you can buy, sold in limited editions and fetching upwards of $100 on eBay, repository of all we secretly need and hoard, but fear to own up to in public). When my wife cajoles me to make room for groceries in the trunk, I resist it. I can leave the jumper cables, the spare tire, or the jack at home. How often do you need those, anyhow? I've got AAA. Clearly it is necessary to be able to outfit up to ten friends who could conceivably join me for any given round at any moment with six discs each. This is simple courtesy. It is important to open up my trunk among non–disc-golf friends and see their baffled stares at my neat set of bins of discs (organized by their flight pattern, color, and type of plastic). At least I don't collect dolls, or human remains, or hair samples from friends long gone, or something truly odd. I like the attention, though it often comes in the form of ridicule, and I won't change my life to avoid it. Maybe we can chalk this up to a combination of exhibitionism with obsessive-compulsiveness and a touch of schadenfreude.

Or maybe it is a serious lack of impulse control, something that has long been a problem of mine (see the crime, the "Cranbook" essay in this book). There is something exuberant about the feeling of new plastic, especially the Champion Line plastic (Innova's name for it, whereas Discraft calls it Z-plastic), which is sometimes translucent, fluorescent, candy-colored, and just a little bit sticky—it feels Space Age, made for the air, made to be accelerated by my arm out into a fairway as it stretches down a hill into the open. And materials advance each year: Innova just introduced the new superstable star plastic, like the Champion, but better in cold weather, and Discraft responded with their similar ESP plastic, which is about the same, albeit with a sweeter name. As such I covet, am a massive sucker for it, and if I go into a disc store, I am guaranteed to come out with at least one new item for the arsenal. I suppose this is how car buffs feel about some sweet new ride they are about to pimp. Or gun freaks fondling their new ceramic Glocks. This is the lure of technology, of having the newest, coolest, most advanced equipment because each new thing opens up a hole in the world that you can step through and become a new and better you. Not all disc golfers are seduced as often as I am, but such is the province and the genius of the nerd. It is human nature—I am resigned.

So if my right arm is far stronger than my left from repeated use, who cares? Just because I have the students in my business-writing class work on proposals for a disc-golf course on campus doesn't mean I care less about their futures. A disc-golf course would improve their futures, make this whole campus, this whole world a better place. When I was still in school, I would ditch nearly any class to get in a round if it was suggested by a friend. I did fine, after all: summa cum laude is for chumps. So I subscribe to the glossy *Disc Golf World News* and keep copies in my bathroom. I refuse to hide them under *Harper's* or the *New York Review of Books* without the proper intellectual shame: Where's the harm in that?

Several stereotypes are true: a lot of disheveled-looking people smoke a lot of pot while playing, hidden in the woods like elves. I rarely get through a round at one of my four regular courses without being offered a joint. This is real generosity. The premier local course, the pretty good 36-hole Brewer Park, will find 200 people hanging out in the parking lot on summer-league nights (of course there are leagues for this; the one I play in is named—embarrassingly—the Grand Rapids Dogs of Disc; if you prefer, you can play with the Chain Smokin' Chicks), Def Leppard or Cinderella streaming from the windows of pickup trucks and Trans Ams, beers in hands nearly all around. Some come to party, whereas I come to play (though I rarely turn down a proffered beer: that's just rude). The Professional Disc Golf Association (PDGA—add .com at the end of it to find their web site and much evangelism about the game) touts disc golf as being open to anyone from any economic class or background. Hence the Trans Ams. Hence Cinderella ("That gypsy road won't take me home . . . I drove all night just to see the light"). Yes. At my weekly league nights, several guys call me The Professor since there aren't many college profs who play the game—and this is shameful, considering how many courses are and should be built on college campuses. A friend of mine in grad school had his composition class meet on the course one spring, where he lectured briefly as they followed him on his round. Something to admire, to aspire to, this perfect wankery. Another friend, once grad student and now sort-of-stunned professor, plays disc golf between his classes, since his office at St. Olaf (Minnesota) overlooks the campus front nine, which is a tight little course. He is the master of his own domain, and you can challenge him if you visit. He will meet you on the first tee. You do see smart folks out there, though: I used to play in Iowa with a guy finishing up his PhD in soil sciences who was a world-class if self-promoting player, also excellent at chess. He was single, serious, dogged, manic, in pursuit of his obsession. Aren't we all.

I never have a hard time understanding people's geekdoms—whether it's playing the first *Bard's Tale* game on their retrofitted 1985 PC with 16-color EGA graphics, trying to decipher the copy-protection code wheels that came with games like this, memorizing thousands of columns of baseball statistics, writing fan fiction with Mulder and Scully finally getting it on in a drunken and implausible threesome with Krycek, or digging through trash in hopes of finding illegal treasure for the eBay altar. My neighbor goes through condemned houses to salvage chunks of old crown molding and molding woodwork: I have some sympathy for him. I have accompanied him through the blocks of houses condemned and recently vacated by transients and immigrants just South of I-196 in Grand Rapids, Michigan, which the contractors claim will soon become a medical complex or, more likely, a strip mall. I've gone through Michigan Bell trash cans in hopes of finding abandoned telephone-system manuals and equipment. I know the men (and women) who obsess about University of Alabama Crimson Tide football games, that long and hot tradition, who show up by the hundreds of thousands for home games against Auburn, LSU, or Tennessee. I had season tickets as a student; I sold my tickets on eBay for $300 or more for some games, even during the dark NCAA probation years. These obsessions are good in their own way. I can get behind them. I can see that there are pleasures in nearly everything if taken seriously enough.

It frustrates me to have to explain the root of my obsession, to tease it out, lay it on the table, and take it apart. And I'm not sure that we can ever see ourselves from enough distance to comprehend our actions. Nor should we. Being deep inside of something is good—maybe we need to lose ourselves.

So, then: why? Why really? There is real aesthetic pleasure in playing a round with my few remaining good friends from college in the morning, before most people are up and after those who are unfortunate enough to be up and not to be us are already at work. I love the sight of the disc in the air, its predictable motion as it flattens and turns, then turns back (the term for the proper flight of a well-thrown driver is an S-curve because of its shape, though it's sometimes called a helix) around a stand of trees toward the Mach V basket made from chain-link steel. The combination of that flight and whistling sound as it rushes by your head is beautiful. It is power. The power is addictive—and this is the first sport, game, or recreation that I've been *really* good at, so there's that, too: the pleasure not of mastery perhaps, but at least of an easy competence. There is the appreciation of course design, of a really well-designed hole like Grand Rapids, Michigan's Riverside Park number 15, 200 feet out to the basket on the end of a peninsula with the lake cresting up around it, the green slick with goose shit (the geese love this hole above all others in spite of the incidence of flying plastic which—

to my thinking—would be a deterrent). Or hole 21 (out of 27) on Cedar Lake, Indiana's course, a hole that stretches 410 feet around the edge of a lake, protected by trees on the left, and tempting you to go long over water for the green, for the birdie, or else to lay it up, play it safe for par like the chump you are, the chumps we all probably, eventually are. Risk and reward. And the sound: not the anticlimactic *plunk* of the ball as it drops quietly out of sight into the hole, but the satisfying crash, the ring, the *ching!* of disc on chain. Aesthetics, appreciation, other things that start with *A*. Yes. But also there is fellowship: the game's played best with friends, the friends I've made out on the course (something about the game lends itself to talk more than ball golf does, and the people are nicer on the disc-golf course). And there's nature and a controlled isolation, the pleasure of that good walk spoiled, what I imagine hunters enjoy from being out in the woods, but without shooting the crap out of everything or freezing silently in a tree stand. And there is the pleasure of obsession itself, immersion in the world of esoteric detail in spite of (or maybe because of) the derision of the *patzers* who just don't understand what it is to lose yourself so completely in something, and who cares, finally, what that is?

So in the end I am left with this: the view from the long hole 18 (pro tee—the serious should always play the longest, hardest tees) on Wisconsin's Elver Park course (on which my friend Leonard memorably played over 150 holes of golf in one *Cool Hand Luke* day when he was out against the world on a day off from being the best worker at the worst job at Taco Bell at the East Towne Mall the summer that we lived in Madison), which stretches out 500 feet with a 300-foot vertical drop down a huge hill toward the fields. It's a hole that you can reach with one good strong throw with a chance of hitting an ace, of crushing the plastic directly into the chains with a gallery of potheads, kids, and other malcontents watching at first listlessly and then with enthusiasm (dude! check it out!) as the shot takes on its shape, starts to live up to its design, the proper mix of muscle and trajectory, spin and snap and luck and angle of release, and slopes finally toward the basket. You can feel blood and adrenaline, feel your hopes rising as you listen for the sound of disc on chain, and then the cheer. Now that is something to remember, and a reason to keep playing whatever it is you play.

FAILURE: A MEDITATION
ANOTHER ITERATION
(WITH INTERRUPTIONS)

If there is form, then there must be failure of form

and there must always be further failures

for there always are

in the cellar

some personal, inevitable

some cultural, beautiful

with the beets and the other wrecks of last year's canning

stored in jars.

for years

The Museum of E-Failure, a collection of ghost web sites

collects web sites that, for one reason or another

have gone dead between 1998 and 2003

I have always thought a good project

would be to catalogue and pedigree

the thousands of dead literary magazines

the cast of signs and defunct ISSNs

. . . . smoke traces of what there was . . . .
. . . .
                                                                          .
                                                                          .
                                                                          .
                         what was, was here before this wreck, .
             in this gap, this yawning space, this wasteland .
                          this Butte, Montana, world .
           where sinkholes fill with rain and mining chemicals .
leach into the water, and birds land on the surface of these pools .
                 sicken, turn, and die, and bob there .
                  like leftover bits of punctuation .
                                                                          .
                                                                          .
                                                                          .

. . . . some magazines more recently deceased—like *Partisan Review* . . .
. . . . or *Story,* or the *Prose Poem*—and some . . . .
. . . . dead for many years: *Godey's Lady's Book* (1830s) . . . .
. . . . *Dennie's Portfolio* (1801, as *The Port Folio* through the 1820s) . . . . . .
. . . .
. . . . The *Gentleman's Magazine* . . . .
. . . . (renamed as *Graham's Magazine* in 1841) . . . .
. . . .
. . . . gone now . . . .
. . . . but somehow lodged . . . .
. . . . in our cultural memory . . . .
. . . . or, more likely, in archives . . . .
. . . . where the dead . . . .
. . . . live on . . . .
. . . . as noble gases caught in beakers . . .
. . . . forever ranging . . . . . .
. . . . and waiting for our call . . . .
. . . .
. . . . Bruce Sterling, sci-fi writer and visionary . . . .
. . . . (he collaborated with William Gibson of *Neuromancer*
and cyberpunk fame on *The Difference Engine*—one of the progenitors
of the "steam punk" literary genre) . . . .

. . . .
. . . . has started a project to catalogue . . . .
. . . . forms of Dead Media—the phonograph . . . .
. . . . the eight-track, the telegraph . . . .
. . . . and all those wired creations with futuristic names . . . .
. . . .
. . . .
. . . . and how many times have we heard pundits complaining,
proclaiming . . . .
. . . . the book's death . . . .
. . . . whether online or in print, but yet . . . .
. . . . the book—as form, as technology, as pleasure, as this—persists . . .
. . . .
. . . .
. . . . and we love it . . . .
. . . . even as we love our complaints about it, its unsuitability for
these digital days . . . .
. . . . the growing population . . . .
(a mold, a monolith, a spread in space) of published books each year,
each one special, each one a new voice, an original talent with something to contribute to our world of information . . . .
. . . . and we love to see
books and authors (almost celebrities) brought down, hence our fox hunt
with James Frey, our exposure and excoriation of the plagiarists, our own
homemade mission to search and love, talk about and destroy . . . .
. . . .
. . . . We love wrecks. . . . . we fear / we cause / we are wrecks . . .
. . . .
. . . .
. . . . . The writer Dame Rose Macaulay loved the wreck, ...
. . . . see her near-archaelological/near-anthropological book. . . .
. . . . *Pleasure of Ruins.* . . . .
. . . .
. . . . and the web—ruined, scattered as it is—loves it too . . . .
. . . . *see also* the web site *Welcome to Heart Failure Online* . . . . . .
. . . .
. . . . as if the heart's stop and double-clutch . . . .

. . . . is something more personal—a nightmare . . . .
. . . . cafe with its electric lights gazing . . . .
. . . . out—pseudo-Edward Hopper—to the street . . . .
. . . .
. . . . (the web site's subtitle: "The Website Dedicated to
the Patient with Heart Failure"—seems at the least a strange dedication
considering those patients' prognosis) . . . .
. . . .
. . . . The HFSA—Heart Failure Society of America— . . . . . .
. . . .
. . . is also quite creepy . . . though doubtlessly its mission—to disseminate
information about this brought-on-by-fat, constant American threat . . . .
. . . . is good and necessary . . . .
. . . .
. . . . The celebration of the failure of the central organ of
the body seems a strange project, but now all sickness is a culture, is
a club—*see* Barbara Ehrenreich's 2001 essay in *Harper's*, "Welcome to
Cancerland," on the wonderful world of breast cancer . . . .
. . . .
. . . .
                                                                                              .
                                                                                              .
                                                                                              .

sometimes I just feel played   splayed out   or spread .
                         spaced   in the face of   it .
    the impossible   burst   of everything .
                    punctuating   everything
                                                                                              .

                                                                                              .

                                                                                              .

                                                                                              .

. . . .
. . . .
. . . . *Failure is impossible*—the final . . . .
. . . . words of Susan B. Anthony to the National . . . .
. . . . American Woman Suffrage Association . . . .
. . . .
. . . . I would argue failure is inevitable . . . .

. . . . and obsolescence a kind of accomplishment . . .

. . . .

. . . . .and www.failure.com . . . .

. . . . leads you to *Exponent,* a technical . . . .

. . . . engineering firm—an interesting domain name choice, the failure of the domain to lead you to what you expected—it is a pointer to a ghost . . . .

. . . . an empty box . . . red herring . . . .

. . . . . . or something more sinister (think whitehouse.com . . . .

. . . . that URL that led countless grade-school students unintentionally to porn . . . .

. . . . [this redirection a sinister, ... effective marketing strategy] . . . .

. . . . —this whitehouse.com web site even claims to have "been featured on *ABCNews, CNN, C|Net, MSNBC, NBC-Dateline,* and *Newsweek*", and this is doubtless true, though it was featured as the most famous URL sham in history [any press is good press, especially notoriety] It was visited by over 85 million people—a McDonald's boast equivalent—crows the front page . . . .

. . . .

. . . . and each new crappy movie tells us it is this week's #1 [crappy] movie in America . . . .

. . . .

. . . . popularity a sort of endorsement; the failure of critique . . . . to stick . . . .

. . . .

. . . . like the prefab nineties British pop group the Spice Girls who, on their first exposure to the public, attracted the media's ire: . . . . the British press mockingly labeled the five girls sporty, posh, ginger, baby, and scary; and then the Spice Girls simply appropriated those nicknames . . . .

. . . . and grew . . . .

. . . . into the media megalith they became before they too returned to dust . . . .

. . . .

. . . . and we'll return . . . .

. . . . to failure analysis & engineering . . . .

. . . .
. . . . the failure of form to support innovation . . . .
. . . . to support the content—potential outcome of this essay . . . .
. . . . . [always a possibility . . . .
. . . . and always this self-referentiality, a buffer against critique . . . .
. . . . a cushion against the fall]— . . . . .
. . . .
. . . . the pressure that any literary thing exerts . . . . . .
. . . . against its scaffolding as it is . . . .
. . . . constructed . . . .
. . . . raised up, bit by bit . . . .
. . . . above the ground . . . . . .
. . . . this pressure that builds until . . . .
. . . . the scaffolding is removed . . . .
. . . . and the language stands . . . .
                                                                              .

                                                                              .

                                                                              .

                                                        as is .
                                                      if it does .
                                or else returns to dust, to rust, a passing .
                                          and extinguished lust .
                                                ashes and .
                        the pizza crusts decomposing in the trash .

                                                                              .

                                                                              .

                                                                              .

. . . .
. . . .) . . . .
. . . . My failure to report an accident to the police—inexplicable
now; certainly it occurred to me to do so after I backed into a gas pump
at nineteen: my passenger friend yelled at me to drive, motherfucker,
drive . . . .
. . . . and I did . . . .
. . . . (being 19 and a dumbass) . . . .
. . . . and this ended as you'd think, in a frenzy of ticketing . . . .
. . . . . . though it could have been worse—suspended license . . . .

. . . . (one of the worst American failures) . . . .
. . . . instead of hospital or jail . . . .
. . . . my own highway failure . . . .
. . . . failure to segue successfully to .
. . . .
. . . . . . *Highway failure* . . . .
. . . . *Failure of the road pavement—deflectograph* . . . .
. . . .
. . . . *Investigating road pavement failure* . . . .
. . . .
. . . . *Pavement structural failure* . . . .
. . . .
. . . . *determining cause of road pavement failure* . . . . . .
. . . . *Trial holes and their failures* . . . .
. . . .
. . . .
. . . . —all these engineering sites devoted . . . .
. . . . purely . . . . to failures . . . .
. . . . of forward thinking . . . .
. . . .
. . . . failures of structure . . . . (again the attraction . . . . .
. . . . to force and to form) . . .
. . . .

.

.

.

is this form a failure .
does it get traction against the page .
the subject   the language   does it get action .
or its opposite .
or does it wilt and fold .
in on itself, .
require resuscitation, radical surgery, or a eulogy .

.

.

.

. . . .

. . . . .Consider antiobesity drugs and surgery
options—only (typically) tried . . . .—. . .
. . . . . . after "failure of lifestyle modifications" though increasingly . . . . .
. . . . as you've noticed, it's all about weight loss without the work . . . . . .
. . . . . . (which will undoubtedly lead to some bodily failure . . . .
. . some wrench thrown in the body's gearworks & columns of steam) . .
. . . .
. . . .
. . . .
. . . .
. . . . "poverty as a failure of lifestyle" .
. . . .
. . . . "failure of lifestyle evangelism" . . . .
. . . .
. . . .
. . . . and I celebrate all failures political: . . . .
. . . . witness the *Mondale/Ferraro* bumper sticker . . . .
. . . . . on my Mazda Protegé . . . .
. . . .
. . . . (if I could find one . . . .
. . . . I would absolutely drive an Edsel) . . . .
. . . .
. . . . or the *Dukakis/Bentsen* . . . .
. . . . campaign signs on my dried-up, dying lawn in 2004 . . . .
. . . .
. . . . (designed to aggravate my neighbors . . . .
. . . . and as a no doubt useless charm . . .
. . . . against the political . . . .
. . . . climate and the 2000 and 2004 reported failures . . . .
. . . . of due process and election) . . . .
. . . .
. . . . —. . . . . and there are web sites that chatter at each
other, address this failure—the WWW (itself a failed, retired term—who
still calls it the World Wide Web, or that other chestnut, the Information
Superhighway, thankfully dismembered and disposed of for what we
hope will be forever) . . . .
. . . . the web one big museum of the dead . . . .

. . . . the period after the period after the period . . . .
. . . . and the discarded . . . .
. . . .
. . . . —why does the vast distributed space of the Internet
lend itself to the accumulation, the cataloguing of detritus, the feeding
of the glob, the increase, conglomeration of failures: witness all the discussion groups and fansites devoted to cancelled shows, devoted to
erotic stories featuring the characters of cancelled shows now somehow
finding new life as semi-sexy ficto-zombies? . . . .
. . . .
. . . . . . Maybe there is something in the makeup of the web, maker of its
own dissolving . . . .
. . . . . that rewards the obsession with uselessness, with esoterica— . . . .
. . I used to run a web site devoted to Elva Miller, a musician (in a loose
. . . . sense of the word, or more accurately a singer) known as . . . . . .
. . . . . . "Mrs. Miller" who was either terrible or great . . . .
. . . . —it was hard to tell— . . . .
. . . . who did covers of classic songs, but who couldn't . . . .
. . . . exactly . . . .
. . . . sing . . . .
. . . . (she sounded like a warbling something in the mud) . . . . .
. . . .
. . . . the notes on the back of the LP. . . . .
. . . . (I have mono and stereo versions both) toed the line . . . .
. . . . between satire and seriousness—they never quite admitted . . .
. . . . that they were mocking her, and you couldn't be . . . .
. . . . sure they were or weren't . . . .
. . . . thus her fame . . . . . .
. . . . as a liminal space . . . . . .
. . . . between praise . . . .
. . . . and infamy . . . .
. . . .
. . . . (evidently she appeared . . . .
. . . . on The Ed Sullivan Show a couple times . . . .
. . . . possibly as a sideshow or car wreck . . . .
. . . . though one hopes not) . . . .
. . . .

. . . . and Capitol Records later re-released her work in their "Ultra-Lounge: Wild, Cool, and Swingin'" series that I highly recommend you check out, though her weirdo marijuana-themed album, the gem of her work, still goes without remastering or reissue, hidden in the dusty stacks that dot the booths at record-collector shows . . . .

. . . .

. . . . I would occasionally get people who would come across my Mrs. Miller web site and send me ecstatic e-mails, pleased to find another body in the void, pleased to join the club, the teeming masses of self-flagellating dorks, enthusiasts, these visits doubtlessly the result of some lucky online use of the search engine . . . .

. . . .

. . . . (great leveler, great connector for geeks to find each other . . . .

. . . . exult and sneer and cluster) . . . .

. . . .

. . . .

. . . . . . so I know something about the constituency of failure geeks . . . .

. . . .

. . . .

—as does L. Ron Hubbard, who has an article: "The Anatomy of Failure"

. . . . (of course he does) . . . .

. . . .

. . . .

. . . and motivational speakers swing from the rafters of possible failure

. . . . as spoofed by Despair.com's "Failure" faux-motivational poster with an image of a runner, head in hands, and a caption: "When Your Best Just Isn't Good Enough" . . . .

. . . .

. . . .

. . . . . or think of Wendell Berry's essay . . . .

. . . . . . "The Failure of War" . . . .

. . . .

. . . . I love the idea of failure in art—the failed experiment . . . . . .

. . . . the beautiful wreck, the stalled fragment . . . .

. . . .

. . . .

. . . . all the broken chunks of the Greeks . . . .

. . . . . . not failures of art but failures of preservation—archeological . . .
. . . . and inevitable . . . .
. . . . our inability to get the whole. . . . .
. . . . story . . . .

.

.

.

a kind of intermittence .
a breaking up of radio wave .
of electronic wash .
and signal .
meaning itself winking out .
against a background of stars and static .

.

.

.

. . . . —but there's mystery there . . . .
. . . . which sometimes means loveliness . . . .
. . . .
. . . .
. . . . (other times it just means continuing mystery) . . . .
. . . .
. . . .
. . . .
. . . . I didn't fail any class in any school that I actually attended—
though there was a slough of failed tests due to disciplinary difficulties,
and minor instances of plagiarism . . . .
. . . .
. . . . that now I regret, since plagiarism is the writer's greatest failure . . .
. . . .
. . . . —a
plagiarized book report, copied from the back of a Hardy Boys book,
which was my first official publication . . . .
. . . . in the *Daily Mining Gazette* . . . .
. . . . the daily paper of Houghton, Michigan . . . . .
. . . . . (land of closed-down mines and ghost towns . . . .
. . . . land of the industrial wrecks—the buried, angled dredge sticking

out of the Portage . . . .
 . . . . .the thousands on thousands of broken-window . . . . . .
 . . . . indeterminate and no longer functional . . . .
 . . . . buildings . . . .
 . . . . sites of danger, absolutely . . . .
 . . . . and sites of fascination, ...
 . . . . contemplation of loss, of gone . . .
 . . . . of over now and passed) . . . . .
 . . . .
 . . . .
 . . . .
 . . . . —a plagiarized line from a story . . . .
 . . . .
 . . . . in my high-school fiction class . . . .
 . . . .
 . . . .
 . . . . my minor Brad Vice, Jayson Blair moment . . . .
 . . . .
                                                                                        .
                                                                                        .
                                                                      oh come on .
                                                              you've taken it too far .
                                                    whatever pain you have is not worth .
                                            all this: leave it, let it list and drift, jut out .
                                                                     into open space .
                                                              or subsist if it must .
                                                                    and go down .
                                                              in a cloud of doubt .

                                                                                        .

                                                                                        .

 . . . .
 . . . .
 . . . .
 . . . . . So, from the BBC's *Institute of Failure* (a performance and theory
collective. . . . .

. . . . based of course in Britain) . . . .

. . . . the Types of Failure are: . . . .

. . . . *Accident, Mistake, Weakness, Inability* . . . .

. . . *Incorrect Method, Uselessness, Incompatibility, Embarrassment* . . . .

. . . . . *Confusion, Redundancy, Obsolescence, Incoherence* . . . .

. *Unrecognizability, Absurdity, Invisibility, Impermanence* . . . .

. . *Decay, Instability, Forgettability* . . . .

. . . . *Tardiness, Disappearance, Catastrophe, Uncertainty* . . . .

. . . . *Doubt, Fear, Distractability* . . . .

. . . . (a kind of anti-Boy Scout creed) . . .

. . . . but they left out Falsehood and Misrepresentation . . . .

. . . . the sad-eyed dog of Plagiarism . . . .

. . . . or does *Redundancy* cover it? . . . .

. . . . or *Weakness?* . . . .

. . . . maybe the redundancy of form . . . .

. . . . which this essay takes, after the snow essay . .

. . . . in the collection—is this a failure of invention . . .

. . . . or a growing of the concept? Does it break . . . .

. . . . apart? . . . .

. . . . prefigure collapse? . . . .

. . . . Is it a crutch on which the essay . . . .

. . . . or the author . . . .

. . . . perches . . . .

. . . . a treading of water, an

uneasiness to submit itself to analysis? . . . .

. . . . Failure analysis is a branch of Materials Engineering . . . .
. . . . and what a great term—both failure analysis . . . .
. . . . and materials engineering—a loveliness . . . .
. . . . of language moving unfettered through space— . . .
. . . . suggests . . . .
. . . . a methodology, a mindset . . . .
. . . .
. . . . our hundred connotations for the words . . . .
. . . . our terrifying slash exhilarating college classes . . . .
. . . .
. . . . "The Failure of Sex Education" . . . .
                                                                              .
                                                                              .

                                               is this both analysis .
                                                     and anatomy .
                                             or the failure of anatomy .
                                                    a geography .
                                             a graph, connect the dots .
                                    a plot, a plotting of points across the sky .
                                                                              .

                                                                              .
                                                                              .

. . . . —failure as the ultimate criticism . . . .
. . . . we can lever against a policy or subject, that it failed . . . . .
. . . . but again this is perhaps instructive . . . . .
. . . . failed to do what? failed to guarantee results? . . .
. . . . already I am lapsing into business-speak . . . .
. . . .
. . . . and failure as a rhetoric . . . .
. . . . as a personal rhetoric . . . .
. . . . is absolutely useful . . . .
. . . .
. . . .
. . . .
. . . . On weather and its importance in accidents and failures: . . . . . .
. . . .
. . . .

. . . .

. . . . Some effects are quite well known, such as: Ice and snow leading to increases in traffic accidents . . . .

. . . .

. . . . High winds leading to structural failures . . . .

. . . . . . Low temperatures leading to freezing and bursting pipes . . . .

. . . . High temperatures leading to pavement buckles . . . .

. . . . Persistent rains leading to floods . . . .

. . . .

. . . . Other effects are not as well known. For example: . . . .

. . . Increasing the water content of some soils leads to a decrease in shear strength . . . .

. . . .

. . . . As a result, heavy rains . . . .

. . . can lead to sudden soil subsidence and damage to overlying structures

. . . .

. . . Some clays swell dramatically . . . .

. . . . . when moistened, leading to foundation and roadway damage . . . . .

. . . .

. . . . The impact strength and fracture toughness of many steels undergo a sharp decline at low temperature. This can lead to a brittle fracture in cold weather under loads that could otherwise be supported without failure . . . .

. . . . ,

. . . . . . Bituminous materials (pitch, tar, asphalt) can soften in hot weather and, under load, can slowly flow and deform out of their original shape . .

. . . .

. . . .

. . . . —there is a lovely mass . . . . a morass . . . . .

. . . . of language . . . .

. . . .

. . . .

. . . .

. . . .

. . . . The effects of my education's early bottom-out . . . .

. . . . . before I would have gone on to engineering goodness and a high-paying job . . . .

. . . . (my life gone technical) . . . .

. . . . as my parents would have had it . . . . (this . . .

. . . . .a failure in itself . . . . .

. . . . of living up to parental, parenthetical . . . .

. . . . expectations . . . .

. . . .) . . . .

. . . .

. . . .

. . . . Possible failure as a son . . . .

. . . .

. . . (my stepmother blamed her anxiety attacks on my bad behavior . . .

. . . .

. . . which, while in some ways fair, seems—in retrospect—excessive) . .

. . . .

. . . .

. . . . . I like to think that I have not failed too often as a friend . . . .

. . . . though my former friends may want to disagree . . . . . .

. . . .

. . . .

. . . but maybe these are *necessary* failures—failures to keep in touch . . .

. . . . or to keep up with high school friends as distance grows . . . . .

. . . . and as there become fewer reasons to do so . . . .

. . . .

. . . .

. . . .

. . and no essay about failure could be complete without the sauciness . .

. . . . of sexual failure—or its mention . . . .

. . . . though this is not purely confession— . . . .

. . . .

. . . .

. . . .

. . . . certainly American men have sexual failure on the brain . . . .

. . . . or the ad execs presume we do . . . .

. . . . judging from the constant bombardment at the back . . . .

. . . . of *Rolling Stone* or *Maxim* or on television . . . .

. . . .

. . . . I like to think of these as material—the meter, the métier—of

future ruins . . . .
. . . . sites of excavation . . . .
. . . .
. . . .
.
.
.

penis pumps, herbal supplements .
the drugs, the drugs, the drugs .
these sorts of scaffolding for our nether regions .
we must get pumped up .
jacked up .
maxed out, ripped .
erect and architected .
.
we need to stiffen .
pry things open .
arc and make it come to something .
.
.
.

. . . .
. . . . in the way that cigarette ads from the '70s . . . .
. . . . seem bizarre and quaint, overt and overwrought . . . .
. . . . (could we have ever lived like that, we wonder?) . . . . . .
. . . . so this is my tiny arsenal of antiquated failure . . . . . .
. . . . embedded here for you . . . .
. . . .
. . . . Failure, choking, chunking it; lack of success, as noun: . . . .
. . . .
. . . . *abortion, bankruptcy, bomb, botch, breakdown,
bummer, bungle, bust, checkmate, clinker, collapse, decay, decline, defeat,
deficiency, deficit, deterioration, dog, downfall, dud, failing, false step, faux
pas, fiasco, flop, frustration, implosion, inadequacy, lead balloon, lemon,
loser, loss, mess, misadventure, miscarriage, misstep, no go, nonperformance,
nonsuccess, overthrow, rout, rupture, sinking ship, stalemate, stoppage, total
loss, turkey, washout, wreck* . . . .

. . . .
. . . . as noun/as person: . . . .
. . . .
. . . .
. . . also-ran, bankrupt, beat, bomb, born loser, bum, castaway, dead duck, deadbeat, defaulter, derelict, disappointment, dud, flop, flunky, good-for-nothing, has-been, incompetent, insolvent, loafer, loser, lumpy, might-have-been, moocher, ne'er-do-well, no-good, nobody, nonperformer, prodigal, stiff, turkey, underachiever, washout . . . .
. . . .
. . . .
. . . .
. . . . This essay as a failure in itself . . . .
. . . . an aborted exercise . . . . .
. . . .
. . . . if essays have a stated purpose . . . .
. . . . and if this essay has a thesis . . . .
. . . . then it has failed to reach it . . . .
. . . .
. . . . absolutely! . . . .
. . . . and you go, girl! . . . .
. . . .
. . . .
. . . . it has shown a demonstrated lack of success . . . . . .
. . . .

.

.

.

has it borne its load .
has it given birth .
to an entertaining anything .
has it prised, apprised you .
of the important world .
is it now a prize .
or should we raze it .
start again, and let it disappear.

.

. . . . Call it a burn . . . . a bum . . . .

. . . . a doldrum literary creation . . . .

. . . .

. . . .

. . . . but again the wreck suggests the vase . . . . .

. . . . the fragment evokes the once-whole torso . . . .

. . . . the car glass scattered on the road, the flash and burn . . . . . .

. . . . tire-squeal, whiplash, and fire . . . .

. . . .

. . . . and it is maybe better to have failed at this . . . .

. . . . than to have poured it all out on the page . . . . . .

. . . . simple, whole, unmediated, all too easily . . . . . .

. . . .

. . . .

. . . .

. . . .

. . . .

. . . .

. . . .

. . . .

. . . .

. . . .

. . . .

. . . .

. . . .

. . . .

. . . .

. . . .

. . . .

. . . .

. . . .

. . . .

AFTER FORM AND FORMLESSNESS: BODIES, BOATS, AND BATHING

This is my body in the bathwater. The water it displaces is equal to the volume of my body. This is simple if continually impressive physics. Call this body a floater, a bobber, striped and flush with the surface of the lake. Even while in the bath, in my mind I am always in the lake, that big flat, that massive freshwater body. The lake always covers up what it is we want to hide—old appliances, wrecked cars, sunken snowmobiles. Bodies as we see on the shore in *Twin Peaks* or in the river or the harbor in one of many *Law & Orders*, always floating in or coming up from somewhere. An opportunity for forensic scientists to perform their sexy science.

I might be obsessed with bathing, or if not bathing exactly, then the concept of the bath, of a body suspended (or mostly suspended) in liquid, preferably hot and scented. This might have something to do with weight: as you know, you seem to weigh less underwater. When my brother and I were kids, we would stay in one of several favorite Best Westerns when we traveled between our Midwest (Upper Michigan) and my mother's family's Midwest (northwestern Minnesota and eastern North Dakota). At least once a year our family would make the drive, stopping mostly in Duluth, Minnesota, or its twin city, Superior, Wisconsin—both old mining towns, built around the ideas of tunneling and excavation, just on the edge of the Iron Range.

Thus, my brother and I would want the motels with swimming pools, and preferably (for me) hot tubs. We would practice our poor-and-always-from-TV karate underwater, which slowed things down so we could stage a battle, like drugged or drowsy Chuck Norrises. It was easy to flip him since he was younger and smaller. And underwater, the body is more buoyant. It has to do with floatability, the air trapped in the lungs. All those capillaries, caverns, inner spaces.

Not all people can float; several friends claimed not to be able to, on their backs or on their stomachs, à la dead man's float. I have always loved floating. This is due to growing up around and in the water—whether in Minnesota, the land of so many minor lakes, or in Michigan, surrounded by the big ones: Superior, Michigan, Erie.

Weight is a concern. Not like it is for bulimics or anorexics, but it's always been with me. Both the physical idea of it (weight as apparent to us, as mass times acceleration due to gravity) and the experience—a continual problem for a massive number of Americans. I don't mean this as a plea for pity and evasion of responsibility (sad panda, force-fed McRibs for years), but just as a worry I carry with me (think more Tim O'Brien, think of me when I was ten and *husky*—the term makers of clothes for fat kids ridiculously prefer—rounding the bases for what should have been an inside-the-park home run, but only making it to third and wheezing). Maybe this is more slowness than weight, but one connotes the other, as we know, at least in the presence of gravity and air resistance. In a vacuum, whether fat or thin, we'd all wheel equally through the emptiness.

Back to the bath. I can count on both hands the number of showers I have taken in the last two years. Possibly on one hand, not including showers at the gym or while traveling (the quality of hotel bathtubs varies greatly, and this must be taken into consideration when booking rooms, though the occasional public hot tub or, better, Jacuzzi suite, can make up for it). I just like the bath: the suspension and the heat. When I was eight or nine, I would sit inside the bathroom at our farmhouse in front of the heat fan for hours just letting it blow on my back. It was cold outside, all the time, and this was my tiny rendition of spring, my own personal Arizona.

In the last few years, I've become a homeowner for the first time, which is no small excitement or difficulty. The bath was a make-or-break point on several of the houses my wife and I looked at. Of course I wanted one of those claw-foot stand-alone tubs, or else a modern jetted tub, if not a stand-alone Jacuzzi (*Jacuzzi* is a brand that gets its name from the seven Jacuzzi brothers who came from Italy to the United States in the early 1900s, and eventually created jetted baths for hydrotherapy—so technically *Jacuzzi* is an *eponym* if you're interested in the linguistics), though my wife felt that Jacuzzis did not connote the classy life. We turned down several lovely houses that had too-small or too-sad tubs, and the house we ended up with is a compromise, but the bathtub is quite good. The hot-water heater fills it well, time after time, without having to stop to refresh itself.

My love for the bath is part of me: its essential slowness, if not its technology and terminology (all the aromatics—mineral salts, bath salts, bath balms, rinses, body washes, loofahs, exfoliating scrubs—the province of The Body Shops that infest the malls that punctuate the suburbs all across this land, and the occasional visits to Lush, Sephora, those more bourgeois shops) have invaded my life. I otherwise tend toward busyness (if not to say *business,* the realm of those with their MBAs and the perpetual desire for speed and cash, the better life, entertainment, and constant upward mobility), and the bath allows a minor respite. I also love the lightness of the body in the water (so near to weightlessness—that Space Age childhood dream, especially for us once-husky kiddies, bound forever for Big & Tall catalogues—and the water it displaces. Perhaps the fat have always loved their baths, a theory I have not explored but set down here as a random salvo against the vacuum, the margin, the death of the end of the page. Again, that simple physics, that trade-off, that motion.

At least part of the loveliness is in the properties of water itself. If I had gone the engineering route in school, I would probably have been interested in fluid mechanics, flow control, and all the serious calculus that it entails—the mathematics of that sort of physics has always interested me (even if it is always just beyond my grasp), the idea of the predictability of water, the complexity of such a seemingly simple and basic substance. Drink eight cups a day for health, my wife tells me. I try to do this. I try this and I fail: drinking plain water's dull. Give me carbonation. Give me flavor, caffeine, chemical additions.

I can name many instances of my life involving water, as I'm sure most people can. The Slip N' Slide. The runs through the sprinkler. Car washes. Days down at the beach (whether fondly remembered for the sand and the shells and the heat, or poorly, for the massive sunburn and physical awkwardness in your suit among all the beautiful people). Water parks (in the Midwest, this means the Wisconsin Dells). Water balloons. Squirt guns. Jet Skis, waterskis, the piloting of cigarette boats at high velocities in my *Miami Vice* dreams. Playing in the viaducts underneath Highway 41 in all the runoff that leads down to the semipoisoned lake (all the leftovers from a century of processing iron ore dumped into the water). Running hard into the fact of the rain.

This fluid is a fact of life on this planet. It is the ultimate enabler—amino acid blah blah catalyst for life. But look at the loveliness of its form when frozen in cubes, blocks, icicles, glaciers even as they scoured, left eskers in, the earth. Or consider it as steam—again in motion—whether coming off the sauna stones (the Finnish word for this is *loyly,* steam that comes from stones) or off the body. Or the sight of exhaled breath fresh from inside when just introduced into winter. The form of it—so flexible. Powerful. An ultimate formlessness—it takes on borrowed shapes. It fills up basins, pitchers, pools and water towers, everything. Buries it. Water as both (re)birthing and scourge of the earth (*see also* flooding, *see* Noah, *see* all manner of creation stories in world religions).

Water—or its lack thereof—plays a major part in human development. *See* Roman aqueducts. *See also* acid rain. *See* Las Vegas and its preposterous economy. *See also* water shortages in California. *See* crackpot schemes to tow an iceberg down from Greenland to use for water. *See* concern in the Great Lakes states about selling off too much of their water to the arid West. *See also* the increasing corporatization of modern agriculture and its need for more and more water.

The other excellence about the bath is the plunge into it, the pleasures of the first immersion. I use this language when I think about how good literature acts on me (literature as a force that acts on the body). The pleasure of moving from the sauna (*see also* water in vapor form) to the icy lake (or to the snowbank, *see* solid water) if you are serious about extremity of sensation, as the Scandinavians are.

But this isn't (just) an essay about water. Any essay about water must be an essay about form. My obsession (with form, and also water). I know there is a connection here: solid displaces liquid, form displaces form. I am trying to push this into an essay about form and formlessness, about both container and contained. Does language have a form, and what is its container? Is this only marks on white? Is this only displaced, vibrating air on its way to your ear? I am using my hands to mold it as we move further in. Think *meander,* the natural way that rivers avoid flowing straight (they'd rather swing back and forth, nearly parabolic, in the shape of snake trails across the sand—and there is important science that can be deployed to support this claim if necessary).

●

The heaviest physical form in my house is an old school-library card catalogue, formerly from Western Michigan University's library (so says the plate that adorns it like a brand). I know it's the heaviest because we just moved, an experience that a friend calls "continually humiliating" in the appraisal of all one's possessions, their uselessness and wonder, and finally, their sheer mass and volume. A fourteen-foot truck? Or should we go seventeen? Or twenty-four? Or give it all up to one of the moving companies and abdicate our responsibility in every way for relocating the detritus of our lives? The card catalogue is physically imposing. I estimate that it weighs between four- and five-hundred pounds (I know). It is a mass. A beast. A wall. A monolith. My wife and I bought the beast at the Salvation Army and hauled it home. Most libraries, as you know if you've been into one in the last ten years, no longer use them, having moved instead to electronic catalogues, which are in fact more useful. Quicker. Easier. Less expensive to maintain (I'm not sure of this exactly, but one can imagine, and the electronic catalogue is indeed more elegant and quick). Even if you lose the peripheral vision that the card catalogue gave you (the pleasure and sometimes utility of *next*ness, of finding the book before or after the listing of the one you were looking for, the arbitrary wonders of alphabetical order and juxtaposition), it's certainly more convenient being able to do things from afar, and simultaneously with hundreds of others, if necessary. Maintenance is much easier, and I'd imagine these are more difficult to sabotage (I knew a guy who'd rip out the card for the book he wanted—fuck the scrap of cut-up paper and the tiny pencil stub).

Still, the behemoth is capable of crushing me (I think of the warnings against tipping vending machines). What are we using it for? This is what my three colleagues who helped us (barely) move it asked. Not sure yet, we answered. This is what everyone wants to know about it. We just wanted it. How could you not? It served libraries so well for so long (a nineteenth-century invention, with its roots in the 1791 French Cataloguing Code, it is suddenly a relic), it seemed an essential item to have. Technically, we only own one portion of the catalogue itself—a good chunk of the Ps through Q, R, and most of the Ss, excepting the tail end. Which is probably enough to give a sampling of the rigid alphabetical order, its organizational structure, without overwhelming. It runs from *Partisan* through *Social Science,* stopping off at the following places (both strange and arbitrary—a sort of weird little passion play) on the way: *Personality, Play, Plot, Poesies, Poetry of, Population M, Postwar, Power of, Practical O, Pray, Prehistoric, Primacy, Principal, Principles of I, Prior, Probability, Problems, Proceedings of, Process, Program, Propaganda, Providence, Psychopath, Public I, Quar* (a good Scrabble word, one thinks), *Raft, Randolph*—this is the kind of excellent juxtaposition that alphabetical order offers up to us, *Rational, Readers, Readings in, Recherche, Red R, Reflective, Relique, Resources, Royal, Russian, Russians, Sadtler, Saints, Sammlung, Sane, Savage, Schedule, Schriften, Scientific, Scottish, Search, Second Hand, Secrets*—perhaps my favorite drawer of them all (such great potential here), *Series*—the self-referentiality of this one makes for much pleasure, *Shah, Shaking, Sheriff, Sketches, So, Social Class,* and *Social Life.*

This is what I love about it most: the arbitrariness (the strong presence of the form, this force of juxtaposition) produces a sort of poetry out of the alphabetical ether. Empty, it exudes a sense of possibility, of fiery potential. If not for storage, then for imposing order on our otherwise disorganized house, our otherwise disorganized lives. It is a reminder of another, much more rigid time.

The body (odd to call it a body; a body of knowledge? a vessel?—aside from its weight—is rigid and very heavy. Oak or something. What it contains—the order—is also rigid (though different languages and localities have minor variations, alphabetical order is pretty straightforward.) Its strictness creates a sense of comfort for me; I know where everything will fall, where it can be found. It provides a wall, a box, a shadow to push against.

It contains, it has compartments—it forces you to classify, to file away by arbitrary order. The order is important because only through order does it—the monolith of the catalogue, of language itself—achieve a usefulness. Order, structure make it *mean.* The alphabet and the rules of syntax are perfect by definition; they are axiomatic. They are important. They're what the writer has to guide her, a grain, a current, she should—she has to—work within and against.

In fact, though, alphabetical order isn't always as obvious as we think—for instance, in phone books, do we alphabetize A-1 Roofing before all the other As (thinking the 1 as a digit and hence preceding the letters), or as *A-one* (thus placing it under "o" within the As)? (The British Standard of Indexing rule is to spell them out.) But what do we do with *100 Best Stories?* It seems more logical to file it under *h* for *hundred* than *o* for *one.* Do we alphabetize St. Germain as literal "S-T" or "Saint," its logical expansion? And what about international names slash languages? According to an essay, "Alphabetical Arrangement" by G. Norman Knight (published in the book he edited, *Training in Indexing,* MIT Press, 1969):

> It is not absolutely essential for an index to be arranged alphabetically. For instance, in a list of tools in use in a given factory, it may be more convenient to have them arranged, not by a description of each tool, but numerically according to the tools' factory numbers. . . . it is *possible,* even in an alphabetical index, to have some parts arranged nonalphabetically.

This is on the surface counterintuitive, but if the goal of the index, of the card catalogue, is utility, then we should break whatever rules we need to make the thing more useful (without losing the comfort of the structure and its general rules, its methods, and its ways of meaning).

Back to our story. My lovely card catalogue's alphabetical order isn't as obvious as I thought, either. When we bought it, we had to remove the drawers in order to move it—again, barely; don't forget the physicality, the sheer impression of the form—and I finally got around to alphabetizing the drawers (after some debate whether to keep the headings on the drawers at all or to use them for something else entirely). I got it done at last, left-to-right, top-to-bottom:

A	B	C	D	
E	F	G	H	etc.

as one would expect. As we (Westerners) write, as the page moves us. Certainly not boustrophedon (as ancient Greeks, like plows moving back-and-forth across a field:

A	B	C	D
H	G	F	E
I	J	K	L

etc.) and not right-to-left as in Arabic. On completion, though, my reference librarian told me that card catalogues are always ordered top-to-bottom, left-to-right:

A	D	G	J
B	E	H	K
C	F	I	L

_____ divider (on which one might rest one's hands while copying down a call number)

M	P	S	V
N	Q	T	W
O	R	U	X

etc. This is because of ergonomic consideration: index cards are wider than they are tall, hence it's more logical (it's better design) to—referring to my diagram above—pull out two consecutive drawers, C and D, for instance, when they are reasonably close together (arm-length), rather than pulling out D and E in my initial diagram, much farther apart). Of course boustrophedon would have worked well here too, but might have been even more confusing to the masses unfamiliar with the subtleties of ancient Greek.

This was strange to me, not only because of the violation of the near-universal organization of the Western page, but because I didn't remember this card-catalogue-organization method at all. I have used many in my life, before they were rendered obsolete, but you'd think the form, its simple rules, would have been imprinted in me more effectively or permanently. And in this case, it's odd to find myself concerned with a technology of indexing, an old order, when it is in fact indexing nothing. The card catalogue is empty. The terms are only pointers to ghosts. We don't have the library's collection, nor do we have the actual cards with the call numbers and subject guides. But I guess there is a beauty to the structure, the empty vessel (I am speaking both of the wooden shell as well as the order it implies) simply, in itself, to what the form *stands for*. When the lights are out, the plastic sheaths that cover the subject headings reflect little bits of light from passing cars; they look like building windows with the lights left on all night because it's cheaper in terms of lightbulb life to leave them on than to turn them off and then back on.

This is a defunct technology, like so many gone before it. Herman Hollerith, the inventor of the punch card, used the cards originally to help tabulate the 1890 census, and the cards were used for about a solid century, most obviously in the old huge room-filling mainframe computers as a method of getting programming instructions into the machine. The technology is of course hugely outdated (though there are still a few residual machines that use them—certainly some hotel-door locks (ExtendedStayAmerica still uses a form of this) and most famously voting machines and the 2000 return to the language of the punch card, the hanging chads, etc.—and they still carry on as part of our cultural language and memory: *e.g.,* "do not bend, spindle, or mutilate," though I'm sure this too will eventually pass out of memory like dead light from distant stars). Steven Lubar of the Smithsonian Institution has written a nice cultural history of the punch card (this can be found online through Google—the technology of the extending moment—easily enough). The punch card—I have a stack of these, found at a sale at Michigan Technological University, when I was younger—is very pleasing in its antiquity and in the forward-thinkingness of the technology (think of the 1960s conception of space and the future—all this great and steely optimism). The punch card is a form that still carries some minor information (for those who know how to read it, certainly), but also describes an emptiness—another index to another set of ghosts. It is a ghost now of a higher order.

⬤

The other stream that leads into my love of bathing is the Finnish tradition of the sauna (pronounced *sow-na,* the pig, not *saw-na,* the tool, by the Finns). My parents have a sauna in both their cabin on the lake (Superior, of course: why settle for less?) and in the basement of their house. Nearly all my relatives had saunas when I grew up. They were places of refuge from the cold weather, arguably useful in healing and wellness, as well as bastions of a creepy sort (I thought at the time) of unfortunate family nakedness. As of 1997, there were nearly as many saunas in Finland as cars. The sauna—and I mean the traditional sauna when I say this, though I can't think of many real innovations in sauna technology that have caught on—is an exercise in tradition, in the old form. The proper sauna still heats rocks taken from Lake Superior— very old forms, these stones, indeed.

●

This is the stream that runs behind the farmhouse in which I grew up. Brook trout are found in streams like this, as are various types of occasional perch, water striders, and many bits of old wrecks (the barn, abandoned cars, wooden doors, and other hardware deposited randomly into water and then forgotten). In other parts of the country, you might hear about bodies being found in streams like this. Technically, it is a creek or crick. It is on no map. In the summer it barely creeps by the beds of forget-me-nots in the backyard. In the winter it is hidden beneath the ice, but you can still see it moving (a form and yet not a form—or one form of the same material beneath another). In the spring it is all rush and blitz and foam and goodness. When I was a kid, I was fascinated with it—both in its meandering from the source down to where it emptied into Portage Lake, just off our property. I liked it for the usual reasons—fish, bugs, dams, fun: all good one-syllable words important to boys like me. Now I think of it in terms of terms like form and motion, both its form as I remember it (doubtless different from the actual, though the actual form also interested me, and I do remember my annoyance at it not showing up on any maps—those indexes to the geology and topology of things) and the motion out from my childhood to my memory, to my memory of its form (and the way in which the crick formed me). I don't like living away from water, even now. I'm not desperate for it, but the few years I spent in Iowa felt strange to me—no natural lakes within a hundred miles; only a reservoir close to Des Moines that felt so utterly *forced*, so false. This is what happens when we try to create a lake out of nothing. I have an attachment to the form of the crick, if only because I grew up around one. I imagine that this is how those literally raised on the water—on schooners, sailboats, or houseboats—must feel.

My memories offer up form from formlessness—certainly they are more a mass, morass of things than a toybox of specific childhood forms. They find their way into my writing. Is this a Bad Thing, I think, and do not know. I do not want to be a slave to my obsessions. In indexing my first book, *Other Electricities* (which was quite a pleasure in itself), my obsessions became too obvious: *weather, snow, blood, brother, barn, murder, father,* and *radio,* among them. Interestingly not much about the crick, but there was much about the lake. I thought about doing a concordance (and in a way, the index is—by default—a sort of concordance of ideas and characters) of the book just to see. (You can see an expanded, speculative version of the *Other Electricities* index, "Index for X and the Origin of Fires," earlier in this book.) An index can be useful in defusing or at least addressing one's own writerly tics, too. Are other writers different—less fixated, less focused, less stuck— than this? I don't know. I hope so.

Our first and last form, the form of *the body* (*see also* corpse, *see also* remains, *see* whatever's left) is an interesting one. When someone's killed, you used to see those tape marks left behind in the shape of the body, a marker or an index to where the body last came to rest. An outline of a ghost. (Maybe this is an outdated technology, replaced by digital cameras and computer-aided drafting, because they don't show it on *CSI.*) I came to the body late. I came to crime fiction late. I came to mystery stories late. But I came nevertheless. There is always a body. There is usually a woman. There is something to be uncovered. Bodies are found in lakes, under long winter snow, walled up in houses like dead cats, and certainly on television, which is obsessed with bodies. The media is obsessed with bodies (both alive and dead). Look, there's Mary Kate and Ashley Olsen, at least one of whom is almost disappearing in the light! Look: there are the hot twins! So says the male world's creepy erotic fascination with them. The only thing better than a body is *two bodies* that are pretty much the same (one imagines). And the only thing better than sexy twin bodies are dead twin bodies—still glamorous and desirable but now gone so far remote, now the object of a different sort of fascination.

—

This is my mother's body, a topic I do not often write about but always write around. It is like a white taped-off form on the floor of my mind, if my mind can be said to have a floor. It is photographed and filed way back there.

—

A recurring theme in my imagination, and certainly in my literary imagination, is armlessness, amputation: the attenuation of the body due to accident or illness, or the defects caused by birth. Put simply, there is something fascinating about armlessness. There's a great passage in James Dickey's *Deliverance* about the options for accidents on the rural farm. Armlessness is not purely rural, but certainly the varieties of farm machinery offer up ways for the inattentive to lose their digits, hands, feet, or limbs entirely. (There's plenty of this action to go around, as seen in the slaughterhouses, as seen on the assembly lines of my dear Michigan's automotive industry—this is hardly the province of the provincial.) Still, when I lived in Tuscaloosa, Alabama, I felt surrounded by armlessness. There were so many missing limbs. I made midnight ventures to the frenzied zombies who work at Super Wal-Mart there (an ex-girlfriend was even flashed at 2 a.m. in the parking lot while I was getting the car, a shocking experience that I didn't even get to witness firsthand. Who would think that the sudden exposure of the body to another body would be so shocking and invasive? But it is). It was impossible to get out of the store without a half-hour wait in the checkout line due to inattention or idiocy or just plain Southern slowness. My favorite all-time checker was a one-armed woman. She was as efficient as the cool machine of mathematics, especially considering her amputated limb. And I write this with a full sympathy for Wal-Mart employees, having worked as a checker and then in the electronics department (along with a very serious Michigan-Militia-type guy—the whole shebang: black helicopters, assassination plots, and everything—who shortly thereafter became the manager of the Cosmetics section and stopped bothering me) in the store #2192 (*2192 Houghton, Michigan, whoop whoop whoop,* or so our cheer went)—we did in fact have to do the Wal-Mart cheer upon opening, a peculiar ritual indeed, all our bodies lined up and shouting. As a checker, I worked toward efficiency (we were rated by our quickness and our errors, there was a rating and a top-ten-checkers list, which I never made; how did those ladies—and they *were* mostly ladies—do it?). And this is what the checkers do: they drag the forms across the grated form of the laser scanner. This rings up the prices and adds them all together, inscribes them on a form that is torn off and given to the customer. Then we—Tetris-style—fit them in bags in the most efficient way. It is always worth doing a job efficiently. It is, as we say, good form.

This is the body of my armless brother, a fictional character who appears in my work, often on the periphery, and sometimes more centrally. I don't know where this comes from, actually, considering I don't have any amputations in my immediate (or extended) family. I don't suffer from amputee identity disorder. "Individuals with this condition" (which is currently trying to make its way into the *DSM-V* like so many other aspiring conditions), according to Dr. Michael B. First (a psychiatrist involved in Biometrics research), "have a preoccupying desire to become an amputee. This desire is so strong that a number of individuals have attempted self-amputation and a couple have successfully arranged to have a surgeon conduct a voluntary amputation of a healthy limb in order to 'cure' their condition. Individuals with this condition feel that their true core identity is as an amputee. The surgery serves to match their anatomical configuration with their true selves, thus eliminating the conflict that plagues their lives."

I am fascinated with this condition—the desire to trim off a limb, a much more invasive body-modification project (I could never find my way to getting a piercing, or even a tattoo—partially since I couldn't think of anything that wouldn't seem stupid later). Doing this is the ultimate display of bodily control. A friend told me about someone (who works at Jimmy John's, a sandwich chain in Grand Rapids) who has all the Great Lakes tattooed on his back. That is good use of the body's form. I could see getting that tattoo.

Still, the idea of armlessness—or that brand of helplessness that it signifies to me, at least literally (though I don't want to glorify or romanticize it, nor does armlessness equal helplessness ... obviously)—is massively appealing. It's grotesque (think Flannery O'Connor, think Freakshow, think *Geek Love*) and disconcerting in a real and nondull way. I don't know exactly what it means to me, in my work or in my dreams, but the violation of the body's form (a form that I don't hold as high as some—some human bodies are beautiful, but I don't hold them all as sacred, nor do those suffering from amputee identity disorder) is something that ties in here—a physical innovation if nothing else. The operation of force, of sometimes massive trauma, when applied to the body, the original form. It is something new and disconcerting, something exterior to ourselves and near-inevitable, a warning that gives me pause.

Is armlessness related to formlessness, and if so, how? Explain.

I haven't had to explain my fictional brother's armlessness to my actual brother yet, as he hasn't asked me about this portion of the book. Does he feel an itch in his phantom arm at night, I wonder, this fictional arm laying on the floor of the story. This is the problem of writing and the family. Not a new one, I know, but still a problem, nevertheless. There is certainly a slim scrim separating the faux-brother from the real brother, and two arms there to boot. Arm and form are a nice slant rhyme. This is one connection. I know there are others. Armlessness is a lack of control, a lack of ability to shape things with one's hands.

I thought I might lose my arm three years ago, when I lived in Alabama without medical insurance, and I found the lump on my left arm (right around the bicep) slowly increasing in size. It went from the size of a seed to a pea to an eye. At this point, I had it surgically removed. It turned out to be benign, but while I waited for the biopsy results, it was a possibility that crossed my mind, a gruesome irony, that I might soon find out what it actually meant to be armless after writing about it. There is the word *cancer,* the nameless, formless killer, which my mother had. *Cancer* provokes a dread in me that has no form, though it has a root in my genetics, in my mother's final story. It is maybe the single most modern way to die, and I thought that it might be meant for me.

This is the body of water that means the most to me: *Superior.* (Odd to think of that construction at all, of *water* as *body.*) This is the body that my father's father used to ferry loads across. He was captain of, among others, the boats *Straits of Mackinac,* 1928, capacity of 56 vehicles, and the *City of Petoskey,* 1940, capacity of 105 vehicles—huge bodies in themselves. We call them (boats, cars) *she.* We think about them in their capacity to bear loads. His body and my grandmother's body brought my father into the world in 1945, twelve years before the erection of the Mackinac Bridge.

My grandfather's body is a body I never grew to know (he died before I was born). All these bodies—these forms—have been laid down in the past. They lie beneath me like those dead in the mines. Those whose bodies were never recovered. Those who died in the construction of the Mackinac Bridge (who fell a thousand feet into wet concrete or suffered other awful fates in the name of civic or financial progress, innovation), the bridge that put my father's father out of business. I don't know what he did after it (itself a massive—and certainly impressive form) was erected, opening to traffic on November 1, 1957, thus making the ferry boat, his technology, his livelihood, outdated, obsolete.

The body of *Superior* holds many of the wrecks of boats—some sunk intentionally as wrecks designed for divers, some sunk in bad weather, without intention. I think of Adrienne Rich. I think of the *Edmund Fitzgerald.*

I love the water's ability to cover over, the ability of its skin (odd to think of it as *skin* but I do: water as body, body as water) to immediately distribute the force of impact and submersion over the whole surface, to cease its ripple and register the entry no more. It swallows up. It consumes and covers over. It barely registers our presence. There are things bigger than us.

There are so many bodies.

They pile up and are compiled.

They are in the soil. They will eventually become oil or coal if compressed enough. If we think about them enough, their forms are with us, hovering in memory around us.

&

I admire those who can control their bodies, control the inflation or deflation of their form. Reading about actors gaining or losing sixty pounds for a role, I find this nearly unbelievable. (My brother is good at this—his ken for control probably; at times he is obsessive when he works out, at least when he has the time to do it; he fluctuates forty pounds down or up; he quit smoking several years ago after years of smoking while chewing tobacco while wearing the patch. This is a serious craving for nicotine we're talking about, but one day he just quit completely, impressing me—I can't quit anything once I've started it.) Probably this is because I enjoy food. A certain amount of gluttony goes down well with me. It might be a lack of self-control or an enjoyment of muchness. I like what the world has to offer my belly. Even more than food, I like—am perhaps obsessed with—beverages. Maybe this is an oral fixation. Or a continuation of my interest in flow control, in fluid dynamics, in water. But I like nearly any beverage. My caloric intake consists of more beverages than nutritionists would likely recommend. Alcoholic or not—there is a pleasure in the sip, the gulp, the effervescence, the color in the glass. I require both juice and coffee in the morning, Coke or Diet Coke (sometimes Fresca) throughout the day. Possibly mineral water, which those on the East Coast call *seltzer*.

●

This is my body, allegedly 70 percent water, in the bath, displacing water equal to my mass. For someone who is as interested in water as I evidently am, I don't like drinking it much, at least water unmodified by carbonation, or sugar, hops, aspartame, or Splenda. I can't bear to drink straight water with a meal. Of course I drink it after exercise, and reasonably otherwise throughout the day, but this is more out of obligation and an awareness of necessity than enjoyment.

These are the teeth part of my body. As you know, I am concerned about the state of them. My teeth have been problems for years (*see also* "Fragments: On Dentistry" elsewhere in the book). They are ground down without my knowledge in the night. My cross-bite makes me a grotesque, a sort of aberration.

I had thought—until the Chick-fil-A incident—that my teeth were a hard form, that they were nearly unstoppable, that they were bigger than God or the humongous fungus (a lichen, the biggest contiguous living organism on the planet, in Upper Michigan). Evidently they are not. The body—the first and most important form, the reason why amputation, body mutilation, birth defects, the tradition of the aberration horrify and consume us, as it's genetically in us, I guess, to abhor the butchering of the form—eventually betrays us. This is one of many stories that comes with age.

It must also be in us to experiment with form, with the body, with what it does or can be made to do. It is in this way like language, alphabetical order, my card catalogue, sex, narrative, physics—all these bodies stacked up on top of us like atmospheric pressure bearing down on our every thought.

There are bodies—or ghosts, the forms of bodies without the content, signs for people and things that have evaporated years before—behind us and surrounding us. They wait for our inevitable decay and erosion down to water, finally away from form. I stand in crowds at night waiting for the ball to drop to signify the coming of one more new year. There will soon be toasts and cheers. Many beverages to drink, to pass through the mouth, the gateway to the body. There is that body in the water, washing slowly up to shore. It is waiting for the television cameras to come upon it, to record its form on film, in bits, in everlasting light. Maybe this is as good an ending point as any. Think fear of death as fear of entropy, as the fear of a final decomposition, formlessness (or at least a final shift in form—we go from one to none, or one to many, depending on your beliefs). Think that this is how the physical laws of the universe tell us it always works, that form requires a constant effort, a continual push against the wall, a finger in the dike, and thus by this push against the wall, this constant plugging of the hole, the swells, our shelter from the squall, we are shaped and we are finally—sort of—saved, if not loved.

THE BIG AND SOMETIMES COLORED FOAM: FOUR ANNOTATED CAR WASHES

First there is the locking into place, that guiding of the wheel into the locking mechanism, the brief terror—have I done something wrong? will the axle bend, or further, snap? will I have to bring my car back to the shop yet again, my tail between my legs, and beg for some understanding and a repair bill mercifully under a thousand dollars?—and then the reassuring motion, and then we're off into the complicated machine with its towers of bristles and spinning brushes, its fusillades of artificially colored foam dripping from everywhere onto my car, and it is sort of totally great.

This is the automated car wash as it stands today, one of many modern things we do. Although it is true that my father (many fathers, doubtlessly) eschews them in favor of the coin-op self-operated types (you know those massive garage doors, the serpentine mesh of hoses, the array of options you get to navigate in search of the gleaming finished, clean and waxed car you know that you deserve, that car which will emerge after five or six dollars in quarters and that timer going down and being replenished several times), or, better, the hose at home and chamois cloth, the elbow grease and Turtle Wax. Our fathers, who art serious about their cars, will henceforth, as they have in days past, wash them by hand. Forever and again, amen.

As you know, there are several types of car washes: self-service (coin and hose and timer); hand-washing (done entirely by hand, though not necessarily your hands; often these are done to raise money for various activities; think Boy Scouts, think girls in bikinis wielding sponges like we see on late-night television or in our dirty dreams); exterior rollover (you drive into the bay, and instead of the car moving unassisted through the tunnel, the machinery moves over you in the stationary car; this still gives the impression of our forward motion through space); and exterior only/conveyor (lock in your wheel and the conveyor belt pulls you through the tunnel of car-wash love). Within the final two categories, there is one further subdivision: these machine-driven washes are either touchless (using high-powered jets of water) or cloth-friction (using soft cloths and detergent).

Can I tell you how car washes work? We'll use a cloth-friction car wash: initially you drive into the *correlator* (which guides the left tire into the conveyor belt that will drag you through—this is omitted of course in washes that instead of moving the car, move themselves around the car—and note its great mechanical name); you go through the *pre-soak* (designed to loosen dirt with chemicals and water), then a *mitter curtain* (loose foam strips) that hangs loosely from the ceiling. A *foam applicator* applies jets of soap, which is then moved around by huge *scrubbers* (sometimes wraparound washers that move around the front and back of the car). Often this is followed by a high-pressure *washer* (a system of water jets that spray concentrated streams of water onto the car—the pressure produced is often in excess of 1000 psi, easily enough to knock you over, hence walking through car washes or leaving your windows open is a seriously bad idea). Then, in areas where there's a lot of snow (and hence salt buildup on the cars), an *undercarriage-wash* applicator. All this is cleaned off via a *rinse arch* (sometimes there are several staged throughout the wash, depending on how complicated the process is), then the *final rinse* (this is the only place where car washes are required to use clean, nonrecycled water—otherwise, most washes recycle their water to save money). If you sprung for wax, you'll go through the *wax arch* (often wax is applied by a series of applicators with foam wax), and finally you regain control of the car as the conveyor pushes you out, and you go through the *dryer* (like a massive set of hair dryers, admittedly covered by a silencer, like on a gun, to reduce the too-big rushing sound). Sometimes this is followed by a hand touch-up, though these are becoming rarer and rarer as many car washes are now all-automatic, new revenue streams for gas stations.

One of the pleasures of the automated car wash is in being the subject of so much engineering (none of it the mind-boggling, ooh and ahh, Silicon Valley–type, but still these techniques and machines are the result of almost a hundred years of research and innovation, the lifework of who knows how many people). Richard Spikes (an African American, unusually, considering the mostly white birth of the car in America) invented the Automatic Car Washer in 1913 (he also invented automobile directional symbols, an improved automatic gearshift, and the beer-keg tap). The first car wash, called *The Automated Laundry,* was opened by two Detroit men in 1914. So we are coming up on the centennial of the car wash in less than a decade. There are nearly a hundred years of successive innovations bearing down on you every time you glide inside the garage-door opening and let go of the wheel for a while.

The automatic car wash is by far my favorite. I eschew the hose and hands. I dislike the constant pressure of the diminishing timer (that signifies in itself an inevitable diminishment of pressure) and the constant feeding, the stream of coins into the slot. In short, I suck at it. I don't want to take any responsibility at all for this task, aside from choosing Ultra Wash #8: Achilles' Shield and Wax So Bright That the Sun Will Blind You When You See It Blazing Off Your Car And This Will Help You Crush Your Enemies And See Them Driven Before You. I have always loved going through the automatic car wash—this was an occasional childhood pleasure with my dad. I close my eyes. I pretend I am in space. I am not in my car but somewhere else: somewhere strange and better. I am caught in memory, in reverie. Or, I am in my car, but I am also someplace else, being caressed by massive brushes and jets of foam, in a sort of automatic constant motion reminiscent of the womb.

We are in the century of the car and of the car wash. An estimated 75,000 car washes exist in America as of this writing. This is my experience with four of them.

Wash One: Cascade Soft Cloth Super Car Wash, July 31, 2004

I am smelling the "Clean Car" scent that comes off an Arabesque® Wonder Wafers car air freshener. The cost is $1 with my "Super Wash" package from Cascade Soft Cloth Super Car Wash in Cascade, Michigan (one of the moneyed suburbs of Grand Rapids, possibly the fastest-growing one, judging from the number of massive developments going in—all those stories of slightly darkened windows and reflected light). This is the first of my four car washes, a good place to start (according to the studies, car washes do best when the per capita income is near or higher than the state average, and the city of Cascade—think of the dishwasher detergent and the water caroming off the auto body—certainly fits the bill). The soft-cloth car wash is preferable to the laser/touchless car wash in that it is more effective, dangerous, and exciting. Nearly all the serious car washes (washes that aren't associated with gas stations or just tacked onto other businesses) are soft-cloth operations.

It seemed likely that the best car wash would be in the richest area, though I'm not yet sure that this is the case (I've had better). I spring for the Super Package (#3 out of 4 in ascending order of goodness; this package includes Hot Wax, a pre-soak consisting of three well-mannered guys hosing my car down with high-pressure hoses and powered foam brushes, the clear-coat conditioner [not sure what this is, though the sign spells it "Kleer Kote"—and note all the alliteration, the marketing they throw at you]; the clear-coat crystal glaze, the under flush, and the regular exterior wash; as a bonus, #3 throws in the rust inhibitor; if I had gone for #4, I would also have received an extra car fragrance). The wash itself takes maybe a minute and a half. Possibly more. Time slows down inside the machine. This is a conveyor wash (the kind I like the best) with the correlator and all. I can feel the belt jerking my car along (rather violently at first, since I wasn't initially told to put it in neutral and was spacing out a bit in my attempts to get a few notes taken on this experience). The car-wash sign says "Magic Bond / Protectant / Only $3 / Ask For Detials [sic]."

Probably the pleasure derived from the cleansing itself needs no introduction. What could be better than finally getting off the grime of weeks of accumulated salt, layers of insect suicide, bird crap, and who knows what else plastered to your windshield? It is good to strip, to exfoliate, to clean and peel and rinse it all away. We love to clean our pores, our faces. Our houses require closets full of lemony fresh cleaning products. We expunge the germs and dirt and difficulty from our life with WetWipes, antibacterial gels, dozens of soaps. Cleanliness is one of the points of the Boy Scout creed: this I remember from years spent in pursuit of colored fabric badges. It is a pleasure and an end in itself: the sloughing off, the sparkle of the new, the freshly waxed, the scents that connote cleanliness and goodness (even, possibly, godliness?) and order.

I'm not sure how to describe the "Clean Car" scent. Vaguely floral. Certainly chemical like all artificial smells, though not overtly so. The "Wonder Wafer" is a strange marbled blue and gives off an obvious and powerful odor. As I try to figure out what exactly it smells like, I can hear "screamer" bottle rockets going off. Dads across the state drive down to the state line that separates Michigan, land of restrictions, from Indiana, land of explosive power and freedom to blow off all five fingers on your hand, and they return with sacks of cherry bombs, fire-crackers, bottle rockets, roman candles for their kids. This is the last cusp of July, well after the Fourth, and I can almost smell the drifting gunpowder scent. Another bottle rocket streaks into the sky above all the nice new ranch homes with their impeccable vinyl siding and their three-car garages as my Mazda Protegé slowly drips dry.

I like its name. Is the car my protegé or am I its?

There is no building within sight that is more than two stories high.

I imagine I will have no problems finding myself a latte or a smoothie on the way home.

The other options for my auto scent are wild cherry, piña colada, vanilla, and leather. I think leather sounds by far the worst, like Judas Priest, like shame. I asked the attendant my initial contact on pulling in, he who holds a big handful of cash, he who controls my car-wash experience (his name is, or might as well be, Clay)—which one he rec-ommended. They did not have samples. He tended toward cherry, but only slightly. I guess no one asks him that. He seemed taken aback.

The actual experience was filled with sound. From the moment I enter the garage and lock into the correlator, the hoses start up. The spinning, moving brushes start up. There is water in the air, as the two guys on the right side of my car have started hosing down the car before I even get the window closed, before I have time to really think about my options vis-à-vis the scent I will choose. For this new smell will be what I take home with me, more than the rush and blitz of the massive interior vacuums (free for customers, a nice touch). This smell will be my afterglow, will stay with my car now for some time. It will probably make me sick. "Clean Car" seemed like the best bet. Also the most op-timistic and abstract, as if a smell can imply this new cleanliness. And why is cleanliness something we aspire to with our cars? Why not just call it Newfound Righteousness, Moral Compass, or Patriotic Blend? (We'll return to these scents a little later.)

Finally, it is not an unpleasant odor. I think I will like it.

One problem with car washes is that you almost never get enough time to dry your car off afterward. A few car-wash places have guys outside to touch up and wipe down the car, but not this one. The belt pushed me through six different arches of superpowered hair dryers (Tempest—!—brand). They got it mostly dry, but still every time there are rivulets that meander down the back, and when I stop, they always trickle down my new clean windshield.

Later this day I am informed by my all-knowing-and-proud-of-being-a-redneck neighbor that all automatic car washes Rip You Off. This is how he says it, with the caps, with a bottle cap coming off in his hand from his beer. We are discussing things over beers, which is what neighbors do. He had a brother-in-law or something who ran one, who gave him the inside scoop, etc. Do you mean that my Kleer Kote conditioner isn't as impressive as I was led to believe? This is what I ask him. He smiles. I think about quoting some of the studies (that I quoted above), but he is not the kind of man who will be impressed by studies or by quoting, much less the combination. Regardless, I will soldier on. We discuss methods of cooking pork. We are men; we are as one in this moment.

One feature of the Cascade car wash is the blinking, colored lights that go on throughout the wash experience: "Pre-Soak," "Poly-Foam," "Magic Bond," "Clear Coat"—here it's spelled more reasonably. These are lit up brightly. It is like a ride at Disneyland or Cedar Point. Colors are evidently a big part of the experience—we need to be told what we are experiencing to really get into it. The soap and wax is naturally clear, but they color it with dye to make it foam up blue (it is almost always foaming blue, I've found, as if blue is a shorthand for cleaning or protecting power). Because it is blue, and foams, we know it works, is good, is worth the money.

Wash Two: The Auto Spa, August 11, 2004

The Auto Spa is on Michigan and Fuller, an intersection currently undergoing some significant reconstructive surgery. Michigan Street is of course named after the state in which it resides; we find this phenomenon in many American cities. I am not sure why. Possibly a lack of imagination. Michigan Street connects some fairly run-down neighborhoods, including this one; I suppose this isn't inappropriate considering Flint and Detroit and the state's decimated industrial legacy. There is the sinisterly named Capone's Pizza and Sub Shop. Also the Kent County Republicans. A bunch of underwhelming-looking stores. The unimpressive Duthler Foods (also known as Dirty D's). A half dozen fast-food chains lit up at night for your attention. Three gas stations on the same corner. And the excellent Rylee's Ace Hardware store, which I constantly frequent due to my own escalating surgeries on my home.

Home ownership allows a new kind of control, the ability to tear the place apart, to gut and rebuild (or hire those to do this for us). We no longer have to submit to the whims and schedules of our former landlords. Our cars give us a similar control: they allow us to be in command of our interaction with the landscape. Maybe this is obvious. Sure, there is a pleasure in the driving, in the speed itself, but it's in our mastery of the land. We are *on* it. We traverse it. We see it blazing by below us. (How long are those yellow dashes that signify *Pass With Care* on two-lane roads? How long a space between them? They shoot by us, or we by them. The dashes are up to sixteen feet long at times; their length depends on the speed limit, since higher speeds require longer dashes for visibility: this is something we cannot easily be aware of—unless we have the maker's eye for roads, the eye of the civil engineer or the road-construction crew.) We don't connect to it physically except when we stop at prescribed stopping places (rest stops, gas stations, Taco Bells). This experience is designed, engineered for us. We no longer have the intimate knowledge of, or even a physical connection to, the land that our ancestors (though I don't want to romanticize them too much; they were, like, totally old and slow) maybe did, walking over it, literally having to navigate it with the body, on a personal level. Now we have our Rand McNallys and our OnStar. We don't even drive on the ground exactly, but on an asphalted and carefully engineered version of the ground, at a specific grade, with a specific crowning so that precipitation will run off and keep us safe at high speeds. We are in charge here. We coast above it in our cars, road noise and heat diminished by ergonomic engineering and the air conditioner's constant reassuring hum and drip.

I am not sure what to make of the Auto Spa. Car washes are often named entertainingly: a quick scan of the yellow pages in the Grand Rapids phone book reveals the following quality names: Butternut Auto

Wash Inc, Car Clean USA, Classic Auto Wash, The Spray Station, Gleam Inc., Great Lakes Tank Wash. I think my favorite of the bunch is "Gleam Inc," though the "Spray Station" seems like a fine choice, too, with its linguistic energy.

Physically the Auto Spa is quite impressive. It is probably 150 feet long. Length is one mark of car-wash quality, I think. It means that you literally get more ride for your money. Presumably there is more actual machinery involved, more stages of the wash and wax and clean and buff and dry, for one to process through.

I am choosing these washes partly based on their name, or their location, confirmed by a quick drive-by to make sure that they are not self-washes. In my attempts to be methodical, I've quizzed about fifteen people I know for their suggestions as to the best car wash in town. I am surprised that most people don't have any recommendation at all, or they choose the closest place, regardless of other aesthetic or linguistic or engineering criteria. No one is or aspires to be an aficionado of the car wash (maybe it is a dumb thing to be). Or else the people I meet and work with simply do not wash their cars, do not have cars, or do not care. For them, it is all about convenience.

To me, though, the car wash offers more: a release from charge, from control, a submission to technology—we lock into the conveyor belt with our wheel and put our car, our baby, our method of transportation, in neutral for a while—even the term for that lack of gear suggests passivity. We will be children again, doing what we're told, being led by hand through hallways toward a room. We will let the machine do with us what it will, what it is programmed to. This is the automotive equivalent of master-and-servant bedroom games.

And I love the rush of it—the safety of the body in the body of the car, a home or robotic exoskeleton. These big metallic bodies mean safety as well as speed. Huge sheets of foam and water sprayed along and covering the form. The form is outlined in reverse, is nearly submerged, and then comes clean. We come out of it reborn or new, fresh like from the bath, clean from all the different types of pressure applied to the body.

It is a very dreary day in western Michigan. Rain has been coming down in spatters and erratic patterns. I have been watching the radar all day as green blotches have been passing over.

The Auto Spa is not busy, which is not surprising. I mean, it's raining. Most people think that their car gets cleaned when it rains (though this is not true if you believe the car-wash literature; rainwater isn't in itself all that clean, and just water won't clean off the caked-up gunk that's on most cars, especially on their underbodies, where cars get most dirty, and where the rain won't likely reach). I prefer it, though, when business is slow. I like empty bars at four o'clock. I like restaurants at five on Monday nights. I love driving in the very early morning when the whole world is deserted and seems made especially for me. So the wash—this whole building and its employees—are dedicated right now only to the cleanliness of my car. A red SUV zooms by me, cutting in front of me through the wash lot to avoid the congestion at the light.

As it turns out, the massive staff dedicated to my satisfaction consists of only one employee. A young man stands in front in a wet shirt—due to rain, perhaps, or excess spray reflected off the cars. He tells me that I am the third to come in all day. While I was taking notes, just pre-wash, he came out to look, to see if perhaps I might be coming in.

As usual, they have three levels of wash. I try the Super Wash, which is what they call the midrange option. The midrange option almost always suits my lifestyle. I am somewhere in the middle. I wonder what percentage of people go for the midrange wash. I bet it is a lot. This one gives me the Triple Clear Coat wax, but not the Magic Wrap. (I ask the assistant, and he tells me the Magic Wrap adds a level of protection against acid rain. I ask if that's really all that useful in Grand Rapids. He smirks, says no.) Evidently he does not own this place, given his lack of interest in upselling me or supersizing my wash experience. He has, he says, been working there for four years. The wash itself has been open over twenty years, and looks it. The Super Wash does include both the Wonder Wax and the Hot Sealer Wax, so my car will be protected against the rest of the road and the world. It has superpowers, can now kick ass for the Lord. Whatever you say bounces off me and sticks to you.

This car-wash experience is very like the first, except I am more aware of the conveyor slowly tugging me along. It doesn't move continuously, but in fits and starts, like swimming in the ocean with periodic crests. Jerk and pause, jerk and pause. It feels like being held by the hand—suddenly I am again a child—and led to or through something terrifying. It is purposeful, consistent, and will not stop, will not leave me behind.

Also, there is no fruit-scented car-freshener option here.

Is there any way to make the wash stop? There is no chain to pull or buzzer to push. No escape hatch. Of course it's not that long, so maybe one isn't even needed. Can one drive faster through it than the conveyor will allow? I imagine this to be true, but I don't want to test this with my car.

This is more a no-frills experience than the Cascade wash. Although again it is very pleasant. There is the constant buzz then wash of the two different jets of spray (one fast and one much slower), the soft and nearly sexual cloth caress, the slow journey through. It's hard to shake the feeling that it is like a ride. The lights light up like sideshows at a carnival. Guess your weight! Take the love test! But here's one difference between the wash here and elsewhere: whoa, the dry. The network of massive tubes and ducts that blast the hot air out at the end of the experience is really something in the Auto Spa. The dryers are massive—probably four or five feet in circumference. They extend down from the huge generator and fan out to a number of openings that jet hot air at the car. I wonder how hot it is. It doesn't feel all that hot from inside. This scene reminds me of something from Ridley Scott's *Alien* with its fantastic H.R. Giger vision of the reptilian and mechanistic future world. Science fiction is a key component of the whole auto-wash experience (and the pleasure that I take in it). I feel as if I am being incubated and will eventually mature and burst forth like a force into the world.

The exit here is different, too—I emerge back onto the busy and congested street, sure, but first, as the car wash spits me out (or releases me—take your pick of metaphor; they're both apt), I return to a remarkably landscaped and terraced parking lot. Everything here speaks of control, especially in contrast to the street. There are small cacti and juniper bushes with rocks surrounding them, a sort of Zen-garden effect happening here just off Michigan and Fuller. This is an admirable design decision. Within the confines of this lot, I could be in New Mexico or Arizona, if not Japan or in the future: everything controlled and gorgeous and subdued.

While I love them, I have feared automatic car washes for two reasons. First is fear for my car, which gets a little pathological with me: though many of the "Laser-Wash" systems always make claims about their touchless wash, something could go wrong—when we aren't in control, our fear is elevated, hence the fear (mostly baseless, as we've all been told, look at the statistics, etc., but still . . .) of commercial flight. The shiny bodies of our machines may be scratched or dented by the machine with the huge fast-moving bristles, our blue-book-resale value dropping by the minute. Second, fear brought on by my car's always-present flaws. Every car I've driven has been in some way crappy, and though this isn't the fault of the automatic car wash as much as it is mine for my thrift and my love of Japanese beaters, still it's a concern. I speak my cars makes and model names like those of friends. My 1985 Toyota Camry's windows weren't a perfect seal, so the car wash always meant a slight dousing of the passenger side; my 1987 Nissan Maxima, an otherwise excellent beast, had a leaky sunroof, so you'd always get some water in through the half-ass caulking job I would occasionally, fruitlessly attempt to touch up. Along with fear there is a heightened sense of excitement, too. This is a controlled, engineered experience, like a roller-coaster ride or slasher flick. Things aren't supposed to go wrong when we're inside. Or they are only supposed to go as wrong as we let them before we are pulled out and up at the experience's end.

Then, a rebuttal to this fear, or something to weigh against it: a study done at the University of Texas at Arlington by the International Carwash Association (essentially a marketing group that supports the dissemination of trade news in the industry, and that supports occasional research), through a special Carwash Research Foundation Grant (this also deserves a parenthetical—but I've been unable to track down much information on this elusive, though often-referred to, foundation). This study showed that hand washing is more harmful than professional washing to cars' surface finishes and paint ("the average backyard hose is not able to supply enough water along with the detergent action to avoid damaging the car's finish"—while professional car washes use a higher volume of water at once, thus mitigating the abrasive cleansing action; though, they use less water overall, much of which is recycled to save money). This study is backed up by a similar study done by the Technical University of Munich in association with Mercedes-Benz. Maybe aside from the rah-rah-rahs there is something to it. Giving up control is good for us and for our cars and for their resale values. It all makes sense, at least if we're looking for useful rationalizations to get us into that heat and light and foam again.

Upon coming out, both my side mirrors are bent way out of shape. Luckily all cars now have the mirrors that are designed to give (they accommodate our predictable minor driving idiocies), so they are easily bent back. I don't see any real damage, though. And it begins to rain again, once again darkening—though not cleaning—the finish on my car.

Wash Three: Standale Auto Wash, August 10, 2004

The Standale Auto Wash is a member of the Midwest Carwash Association (MCA), one of several regional (the MCA in particular covers carwashes in Michigan, Wisconsin, Illinois, Indiana, and Ohio) car-wash associations designed to disseminate information on new car-washing technologies and to run regional expos and other networking events.

One of the hallmarks of the Standale Auto Wash is their "2-in-1 Good Weather Guarantee," which states that "if it rains or sprinkles / or snows one inch or more before 7am tomorrow [they] will wash your vehicle for free the first dry day [they] are open." If you don't take advantage of it, you can save the coupon and come on back for a free wash when you've accumulated ten of them.

(I have had my car washed here before. This time, though, they don't give me the coupon. Have I offended? Am I undeserving? What the hell?)

Too, as many car washes do, they offer deals for buying a bunch of washes at once. The ultimate car-wash commitment available through Standale Auto Wash is the Yearly Pass (for a daily wash—!). I can imagine wanting to have my car washed every day, like having a personal attendant constantly on call. I will think about making the investment.

Standale is not nearly as prosperous a town as Cascade is. Or if it is, it doesn't show it off for the camera. Loosely a western suburb of Grand Rapids, it would appear that the city is mostly the outgrowth of a series of strip malls that line Lake Michigan Drive, the four-lane highway that leads from Grand Rapids to Grand Valley State University (where I teach, the largest college in fifty miles), and then on to Allendale (technically, GVSU resides in Allendale; it's a dry town, with not much to say for itself, as far as I can tell—the college has taken over, so student crap abounds, except for a firefighters' museum that shows up in many Michigan travel guides), and then for another ten miles to Lake Michigan. Standale has a lot of Chinese restaurants, a Hallmark store slash ice cream shop slash post office, several gas stations and service shops, a Walgreens, a bunch of auto dealerships, a restaurant called the German Village, and the Elias Brothers' Big Boy restaurant. It makes me sad to drive through it. However, Standale does have the Standale Auto Wash, "owned and oper- ated by J, Judy, and Mike Cornell since 1979," according to the web site. I've been through once before, on a day just before it snowed. (I didn't have the heart, though, to demand my free re-wash after the snow; driv- ing in the snow is a constant struggle against salt and corrosion and other drivers, so it barely seemed worth the trouble, and as a Midwesterner, I am not demanding.)

This car wash has a few more options that the previous two. They have six different packages available for purchase, ranging from $7 ("Wash- It," which includes a "soft neo-glide wash," an undercarriage flush, white walls, and a spot-free rinse) through $12 ("Ultimate Plus"—as if any- thing could be more than the ultimate. The Ultimate is only $10 and seems to offer about what I've received from the other midrange car washes I've undergone. The Ultimate Plus has a lot of stuff included (same names, same language as the other car washes mentioned above, with the addition of the "Simoniz Double Bond," which sounds either magnificent or hokey). It is quite a list. I am going to go for the cheap- est option here today, though I've been through the Manager's Special ($10) before and have come away quite satisfied. Does the experience of car washing differ? Not as far as I can tell, except that some of the light- up signs when you go through don't light up if you're not getting all the extra bells and whistles. And will I find myself, as I go through with my economy package, wondering whether I am doing all I can do to pro- tect my car? Am I getting the maximum out of this experience?

The employees always say that the deluxe washes provide more pro- tection: maybe the rain will bead more on my windshield and hood for the next six months? We are, after all, in America. Why get the Medium when for another dollar you can get the Large? Don't I deserve it? Yes, I like the attention of the big package, with its litany of impressively named chemicals as they wash—are jetted at high velocity—over my car.

Strangely, though I'm here on a sunny Saturday afternoon in mid-August, the place is nearly deserted. As I write this, one car is passing me, a gray Buick LeSabre (what a good car name that is—so masculine, yet a little bit French with its *haute couture* connotations) being driven by a middle-aged man. The attendant, strangely, is a young woman, which is a little unusual in my experience. Possibly this is Judy, who was mentioned on the web site. She wears a green Calvin College T-shirt and is very courteous. As I observe, one more car moves up—a black Dodge Stealth. I'd say it creeps up on me, but it doesn't. It is a loud car, though it does have a sexy gleam to it. The attendant doesn't meet this one—the driver just goes right in and the machine begins. Perhaps this man deserves some kind of special treatment? Possibly he is a regular, has gone in for the wash-a-day deal? He didn't even stop to look at the options, just cruised on in. I admire men who drive with purpose.

I have a purpose too. I talk with Jimmy, one of the guys who's on the job (the woman clocked out and just drove away in her Ford Probe— another jaunty and possibly sci-fi name), and he's not particularly forthcoming. I think he's a bit freaked out that I'm writing about car washes (perhaps I should not have told him this). Jimmy recommended the Ultimate wash ($10), which he says has about anything you could really need, though he says that the vast majority of people come in and get the cheapest option—possibly because of their natural distrust of the options, of the sales pitch, or maybe this is because they just don't understand what the bigger packages have to offer. Jimmy doesn't know how old this car wash is (he says his boss bought it twenty-five years ago from someone else), nor does he have much to say about where they get their chemicals—all the washes so far advertise the same brand names. In the office, on the dry-erase board, someone has erased several items underneath the heading "Chemicals to Watch."

Several cars are now coming in and being processed through. This is the first car wash I've actually had to wait for (while I was talking with Jimmy, a Mercedes C220 with the Jesus fish on the bumper ducked in front of me—it's great how even our bumpers offer us a chance to stump for, to signify, our ideologies).

I am in. This time the smell is much different—fruity (from the outside—not the interior car smells that you can put in; they omit this olfactory possibility in its entirety). Rainbow-colored foam (green, yellow, blue, and red) is sprayed on the car. It is half gorgeous and half Chuck E. Cheese. The colors mix on the windshield and wend their way down. Intermittent jets blast it off. It is hot in here, more so than in the others. Again, the multicolored lights come up, informing me of the chemicals that I am being blasted with. One sign on the way in informed me of the Teflon protectant being hosed onto the car. The phalanx of overhead fans here are the same as the Cascade car wash— Superior Tempest brand. One thinks Shakespeare, briefly, then that thought is gone. This is the most controlled tempest that is imaginable. There are no car air-freshener scents offered to me in plastic wrap or sprayed underneath my seat. I guess the chemical smell jetted on the car will have to suffice.

And I am out and clean and drying.

Most people get their cars washed alone, it appears. From the twenty or so washes I've just observed, eighteen of them are individual experiences. I watch the people's faces as they come out of the car wash, snap back their mirrors. Some seem completely indifferent to the complexity of the experience that they've just endured. It is a chore to wash your car, they nearly say. They are glad to be done for the month. Or perhaps the year.

Some car-washees come out smiling (like me). They are pleased. It is good to wash your car, they nod to me as if to say. A couple in a Ford Explorer looks excited to be alive (moreso the woman than the man). Their car gleams righteously in the sun as they drive away, accelerating back onto the street through the construction and out toward the lake where their afternoon awaits them. I am glad for them, for their appreciation of our shared experience. And it is a shared experience in that we have all gone through it, though rarely as a group. We do it individually, but I think everyone must respond the same way inside. When you are inside, you are inside. It is all oohs and spinning and excitement. When you come back out, well, that's something else entirely; get your game face back on.

One man in a Dodge Ram 1500 double cab gets out of his car when he comes out, does a walk-around inspection, nods his head as if he is approving cuts of meat. He seems to be looking at one particular area that must have had something awful on it before. He appraises the work, is evidently satisfied, and drives away with a faulty muffler roar.

About this reentry into the world: the Standale Auto Wash hasn't given much thought to the experience of the Exit. There is no landscaping, no lovely rock arrangement. This is emblematic of the town, perhaps, which is straightforward, undesigned. You are in and then you're out. The car wash exits right onto the main drag (a vestigial bit of slang, isn't it? I think of sixties culture and racing for pink slips, jalopies and thoughts of the Beach or Hardy Boys), facing the Day Break Laundry and a crappy bar called Shots, where the S is made up of two shot glasses.

The Exit is more important to the whole car-wash experience than some people think. For a few minutes you're in a world unlike this one—you are in the hands of an awesome and big-ass appliance—then you emerge and are released. This reentry into the world should not be too harsh, too quick. I don't like to be just spit out and dropped back on the street. Where is the denouement? Where is the afterparty and the cigarette in bed? I like a bit of wind down, a little safety net. Some minor decompression. And I definitely prefer to be moved out by the conveyor rather than to have to ease my own way out through the blasting air.

I say hello to a man in another Dodge who sees me watching him. We wave, we share a moment. Two teenaged girls walk by with matching dogs. They are in no hurry. One is wearing a T-shirt that reads *Fresh* across the chest.

Wash Four—Southland Auto Wash, August 25, 2004

How much can one wash be different than another? The Southland Auto Wash thinks of itself as a different breed of wash. For starters, they have a bevy of attendants who greet every car that comes in. I count five (four men, one woman—always only the single woman) waiting in the Full Service lane when I come in. It is remarkable that there is even a Full Service lane to begin with. There are few cars, since it's a humid, overcast August day that smells very much of impending rain. A guarantee is advertised outside: "Clean, Shiny & Dry or Rewash Free," and on the whole, this looks like a very professional operation. The building is much the same as the first three—long and thin. The exception is that there are two stories involved here, perhaps some administrative offices.

The Southland Auto Wash is in Wyoming, Michigan, yet another suburb of Grand Rapids (I could only find one automatic car wash in Grand Rapids proper—the phenomenon of the car wash seems to be made for the suburbs, where cars are a natural fact of life and three-car garages are increasingly *de rigeur* if you care about resale value, as my realtor recently informed me). The city is even less attractive in many ways than Standale. At least Standale has an excuse for itself—it is *on the way*, to the lake, to GVSU. Wyoming seems to me an end in itself, but an unfortunate one. It is mostly sprawl and commercial jumbo-ism. Everything is big and slightly run down. There are some stores you would expect, except that here we see their less classy version: Doctor Zzzz'z Mattress Center instead of Ethan Allen; Tabalooga! furniture in-stead of Pier One. You can find the Southland Auto Wash on 28th Street SW right past the Bangkok View Thai restaurant and the bizarrely fu-turistic Wyoming City hall, which is all glass and chrome and forward thinking (the building stands in front of a huge water tower that also reads WYOMING in big block sans serif lettering). They think Civic Duty. I think *Blade Runner*.

The car wash is across from a Value City furniture, a Fazoli's (a cheapie fast-food "Italian" place), and a Peter Piper Pizza, whatever that alliterative hell has wrought. On the whole, this streeth—28th Street—is not a street I'd like to drive down often. It is probably the busiest street in the Grand Rapids metro area, connecting the west side with the east, eternally clogged and under construction, which never seems to ac-complish much. I think of Kafka. It runs along the southern edge of the city over to the eastern area (the posher suburb of Kentwood), though over there the strip is equally obnoxious, if more upscale (there, you'll find your Ethan Allens and Pier Ones). So it's even more surprising that this car wash turns out to be the best.

This is a much different experience than the others (in the business jargon I learned in school, this is a new car-wash paradigm). Instead of riding through the wash with the car, you turn the car over to the attendants, who detail it (this service is optional, but recommended) and send it through alone. I choose a relatively cheap package, turn over my car to them, and wait in a quiet, air-conditioned corridor inside the building (this explains all the additional office space) while my car goes through the wash. There is a wall of windows to watch your car go through. I think of the operating table as seen from the observation room above.

All this makes for a strange experience. For $14, the attendants detail the inside of the car nicely and add an air freshener. They only have three official options here—New Car, Cherry, or Lemon. I wasn't sure which to pick, so I asked the red-haired attendants (all the front-end attendants have red hair, strangely: perhaps they are related) for their recommendation. Both Lemon and New Car got votes of confidence, so I opted—after briefly waffling—for New Car (I have a problem with artificial-food smells; I always want to consume them—shampoos, in particular—when I am hungry, and then I gag and spit and am annoyed; then one more time I damn this chemical witchery). As it turns out, they gave me both, so there's an odd combination of new-car and citrus smells. It is half tasty and half revolting. Although this does keep me from consuming the scented wafer (even this term makes me want to eat it), which is for the best.

As I stand in the hallway, it becomes obvious that the Southland Auto Wash is a friendlier, more personal operation than the first three. The owner, Bill Ellis, is on the premises to greet the few folks who come through. This is part of his business strategy, I'm sure. Framed photocopied articles about him and the business adorn the walls. I overhear him talking with an older man who preceded me (who is evidently a regular, since he's got the frequent-flyer card) about a storm coming in from the Southeast. I am sure that this is true. It's been awful weather, humid and stopped up for days. Southland Auto Wash has received "Car Wash Beautiful" awards, too, from *American Clean Car* magazine, whatever that is—both are also tastefully framed and on display.

Sometimes I want to tear this whole manufactured world up, to burn everything down.

Other times I want to consume it, embrace it all, mouth open, eyes back like *Pac-Man.*

Signs abound inside. I read them, as I don't know what else to do with myself—for once, it feels as though I am not involved (though my actual agency in the previous car washes was no different, still, being inside felt like a proper collusion, a sense of solidarity with my car). I wait for my car to be queued up and notice that this car wash uses several different technologies, among them the NEOGLIDE Wash System from Kirikian Industries ("Treat your car to a NEOGLIDE wash today! NEOGLIDE is gentle to all types of vehicles. NEOGLIDE has a phenomenal brightening effect on painted surfaces. NEOGLIDE . . . the latest wash technology for today's new generation of vehicles"), which is a softer foam type of spinning brush (as opposed to cloth). It doesn't seem remarkably better than cloth to me on first investigation, but the management provides samples of both materials inside for customers to handle, so it must be a Good Thing. It also comes, according to the web site, in four different colors (blue, red, green, and "reclaim" black with white swirls). Too, it is "revolutionary." This car wash uses blue.

Also, unlike the other car washes I visited, the Southland Auto Wash uses the "Qual Chem line of carwash chemistry: the most advanced in the industry" (again from the marketing material). I don't know if it makes much of a difference to the wash experience, but this involves Q Clean, a "high foaming, deep cleaning detergent" and Q Dry, a "low spotting, fast beading drying agent." The Qual Chem line also comes in a variety of colors (red, yellow, blue, orange, and green—this might explain the Standale Auto Wash's rainbow coloration; it provides another bonus visual element to the experience) and scents (banana, tropical, cherry, and lemon lime, along with custom fragrances—I hesitate to ask what custom fragrances could entail). These are all ways in which car washes can help customize or trick out the car-washing experience.

Finally my car comes up. I watch it ease into the conveyor that will carry it along. After having gone through so many washes inside the car, I feel almost nostalgic for it, like it is a brother or a friend. We have gone through so much together, I think, even though it is a ridiculous idea. It makes me sad to see my Protegé go through by itself. Again, though this is lame on the face of it, nearly everyone I know identifies with their car. Many of my friends have named their cars. We feel loyalty or anger toward them, depending on their repair records and reliability. Cars sometimes become male or female—female more than male, I think, in my experience. I have felt sadness when my previous cars have been towed away to their final resting places. These emotions are as disturbing as they are predictable.

The machinery is—if anything—more impressive when seen from

outside the action. A set of rotating blasters fires water on the car in the initial soaping. Foam drips from a curtain on the ceiling, spattering the hood. Thirteen numbered dryers blast hot air across it as I watch the water bead off. Afterward, the car emerges into the final bay, where another six attendants take chamois cloths to touch it up. This is a pretty impressive operation.

However, it isn't as much fun, as much of an *experience*. It feels clinical or out-of-body, third-person as opposed to first-. There is a videogame element, absolutely. In the interior corridor where you wait and watch, they have a sign that reads: "All new Customer operated Foam Blaster. Southland auto wash now lets you spray your car with foam from right here inside the carwash!!! Southland will still do the dirty work!! This foam blaster is for entertainment purposes only! 1. AIM with the joy stick. 2. Press the red button to FIRE. The foam blasts from the red pipe attached to the ceiling. Wait to Blast until your car is under the BLASTER." (I kept their capitalizations.)

There is the sexual overtone here. I blast my foam onto my car. That's hot. That's weird. That's great.

The other way in which this experience differs from the other is in the sheer variety of products available inside at the counter. By forcing customers to wait inside, they open up new retail possibilities. Armor All, certainly, but also a dizzying spread of car fresheners. One company makes the following scents (here for $.89 in the classic Christmas tree-shaped scented cardboard): Country Kitchen, Apples and Spice, Sunny Citrus, Courage (this one is unbelievably decked out in camouflage!), Rose Musk, Cinna-Berry (like some sort of awful cereal), Lemon, Sierra Winds, Victory Lane, Freedom (!—what does this one smell like? blood or oil or power?), Sport Fresh, Forest Fresh, Raspberry, Fruit Punch, Ocean Mist, Vanillaroma, and Powder.

These could be flavors of Gatorade.

There are a couple other catchy brands for sale: Car-Freshner, Auto Expressions, Ventsations, and Out of this World. My favorite of the bunch is Auto Expressions. Because your car scent, that particular stink, showcases your individuality.

Finally my car is as clean as it's ever been. It's been detailed twice (once by me, who ended up covered in dust that required two showers to wash off, and once by attendants, who clearly did a better job and left me far cleaner . . . in this way, I am happy to be catered to) and washed four times. I've been noticing a couple small scratches on its finish, and it is possible that the car washes have exacerbated these tiny surface flaws (I never noticed them before). If I worry with my fingers at these flaws enough, they will open up, they will eventually split the car or my flesh into its component parts.

Do any of them measure up to my Ames, Iowa, superwash, the ideal in my memory? My memories are filled with apogees, the perfect examples of all things. The best bread (my mother's when I was young). The best sandwich I've ever eaten (pastrami, predictably in New York). The best ice cream (Blue Moon, also from my childhood, from which most of my Bests emanate and exert their strong atomic forces over my life). I feel pleased and satisfied. I wonder if this is an American feeling, if this is how it is supposed to be. I have been serviced with the best that modern technology evidently has, or the best that the Grand Rapids metro area evidently has, and I am (am I?) somehow changed, or buffed, or polished up. It is not a comfortable feeling. I feel like I have been shaped, that I have been somehow made or made over, like I am, legs crossed, sitting in a chair on daytime TV, makeup caked on my face, eyeliner stinging my skin, and me all petulant and ready for my camera time. Still, I am a part of all this—my form is in contrast to all the other forms that lurk behind and in front of me. My body, my car's body, maybe my outer shell, is clean and shiny, and I feel good and new in spite of everything, minor surface flaws and all.

AFTERWORD:
ELEGY FOR TELEGRAM AND *STARFLIGHT*

As of February 5, 2006, Western Union discontinued its telegram services, thus sounding the death knell for one of the first forms of more or less immediate long-distance communication. I have missed this deadline by a week. I have never received a telegram and will now never receive one. Telegrams always end with the word STOP

Is this a failure of myself or of technology? Or a different kind of failure from having rendered service so well that it's become obsolete? In this way success—a perfect usefulness—folds in on itself and becomes its eventual failure. Is it like a star that burns itself gradually away? Is that the purpose of technology, to find its purpose and fulfill it, to, like a booster rocket, exhaust itself and dwindle back into the atmosphere we like to call the future? STOP

There are still telegram services you can find operating on the Internet, but the Internet is one of the successors of the telegram, a successor to the dot-dot-dash technology of the telegraph (like the enduring telephone, the now-defunct bulletin board systems (BBSes) with their own time here and past in the eighties, TYMNET, Telenet, and other data networks, faxes, videoconferencing, IMing, text-messaging, and whatever's next, etc.), and it now provides a gateway to the telegram. It is strange to use the Internet to send a telegram: like pouring one of our Great Lakes into a graduated cylinder or one of those pipettes we used to use in Mr. Luoma's eighth-grade chemistry class while we dreamed of lighting up our friends' hair with the Bunsen burner. As such the telegram has recently been used only for a retro, desperate, or romantic effect: birthday wishes for the old, who might have actually received telegrams throughout their lives; Valentine's Day presents for one's straying lover before a Hail-Mary dinner out. One of the web sites lists a number of marketing ideas, claims that research shows that consumers will discard birthday cards but will keep a birthday telegram. Extend this to the idea of making an impression. That's what they do. It costs $20 or more, depending on the level of service and romance you require. STOP

STOP is used in telegrams because you pay by the word, but each instance of punctuation is more expensive than a word, while the four-letter word STOP was free. So the use of STOP became the norm. Short declarative or interrogative sentences became the norm. Language is controlled, compressed by the technology of its transmission. Because you had to pay per word, per line, your message would be best reduced to its shortest, most efficient form. It is redundant to do as I have and throw down periods before or after STOP; still, this essay is not a telegram (through the long white years of the page I send this out to you) but a shadow of it—it desires only to echo its form—so I only use, sparingly, and with increasing self-consciousness and several capital letters: STOP

Technology enthusiasts know all about self-consciousness and obsolescence. At one point I fancied myself one of them—the geeky, the absolutely hooked, the necessarily obsolete. I love old computer systems, the Amiga, the Commodore 64, the Adam, the NeXT, the old Macintoshes that you can *mod* (modify) to work as fishbowls now or simply clocks. I love the old technology—the spindles of punch cards, corrugated boxes of eight-inch floppy disks (now floppy disks of any kind—and we usually mean the physically floppy 5¼" disks, not the stiffer 3½" so-called floppy disks, when we say *floppy*—are obsolete), 8-pin dot-matrix printers that would hum and perforate every character in every line. I still have a stack of eight-inch floppy disks in my house somewhere. I would love to still have a tape drive in my boxes of discarded parallel and daisy-chained SCSI cables retained from my days as an IBM user (even that term, IBM, which once meant something, is now obsolete, as IBM doesn't even make desktop PCs—now they're just PCs or Windows Machines or whatever you want to call them if you want to call them anything at all). At one point—in the height of my teenage criminal aspirations—I acquired an old Commodore 64 tape drive and was planning to use it to read and write magnetic strips on credit cards. I aborted this plan for several reasons, including my sudden disinterest and attachment to something new in place of it. In one sense, *abort* means STOP

Found in the void somewhere: a maybe-fictional telegram: I DON'T LOVE YOU STOP IF YOU LOVE ME STOP

Many wartime deaths (big end-stops) were announced by telegram. Telegram delivery during wartime came packaged with big anxiety. STOP

As I write this, I get an e-mail from a friend—one of the longest I've received from her in a year, as she's not always so good in keeping up long-distance correspondence, at least by e-mail or phone—which in part bemoans the lack of letter-writing among writers. I've thought this too. Grand Valley State University (where I teach now) recently acquired Jim Harrison's collected papers for something like half a million dollars. They consist of one hundred and sixty-five linear feet of papers, letters, drafts, and other material, which are all now on their way to our archives, where they wait to be sorted through and classified and set aside in piles and catalogued and probably digitized or microfilmed or something (*see,* if you like, Nicholson Baker's book on libraries and the demise of paper, *Double Fold*). I have received a handful of letters from writers who seemed to be trying to start a Correspondence, something that could eventually be Collected into Books and Published by the Few Remaining University Presses in the Future for use by Scholars, if there are any left by the time we're done with the word slash the world. I've received letters in my life written on birch bark, on pornographic stationery, on maps, in handmade envelopes, on handmade paper, on the back of someone's hand then photographed. The writer Michael Martone sends me periodic postcards, showing his devotion to the form. I like the idea of letters very much. However, I hate the act of writing by hand very much, and now I type (though I do occasionally craft things to my then-girlfriend now-wife, or handprint Christmas cards or something fancy). And with the computer the letter seems almost pointless, a discarded technology. I suppose my choice of font is individual, as is the leading and the margin choice, but in the world of Microsoft Word with its helpful letter-expert template and its standard margins, what's the point?

TV forensic shows show us now that every printer has an identifiable toner or ink signature, so there is still a thumbprint buried in its otherwise unremarkable robotic exoskeleton. We cannot avoid identification, though the telegram (and telegraph) was a good start to this—our words coded and repeated sans our own handwriting.

Maybe I should seal my laser-printed letters with my ring's imprint in wax.

Said friend has a job in San Francisco where she is helping to organize and catalogue the poet Robert Pinsky's letters, papers, and other forms of correspondence. She has, as such, acquired the bug for letter-writing, for Correspondence, which is nothing if not admirable, even if I don't have the heart for it. There is something in that—some sort of special, quiet magic. I have these great "letterettes" I found at the Salvation Army or a garage sale several years ago. I don't use them often because I don't think of them that often, and when I do I want to covet them, to collect them (there's always this, the collector's impulse for hoarding and preservation, the unopened shrink-wrap around decades-old toys). They have an old sort of smell. I like to hold them to my nose. Recently I've sent a couple of them out. Given them up. I am trying to use them up, like any good technology, I suppose. The letterettes are the size of a small envelope, the kind that annoy me—you can't just fold a letter-sized sheet three ways and fit it in. It requires two angles of fold, some sort of minor origami, to make it work, or perhaps I am just ignorant of the method. They have various reproductions of natural scenes on their backs, and you address the letters over the scene, writing on the other side (does this cause problems with the post office, I wonder, meaning do they have to be hand-cancelled and hand-sorted? There is so much technology now in the world—that one big dead-letter office—that it is beyond my easy grasp). They come with small gold foil seals, which have dried out, and no longer stick, causing problems when they are mailed. Still one hates to just cover the letterettes up in a regular envelope or send them covered in packaging tape, thus ruining the elegance of their technology, of their form.

I have decided in this moment that I will send one of my last letterettes to her. Maybe she can collect it for her future Selected Letters and Letterettes volume. It would be weirdly flattering—even if something of a betrayal, my private words made public for posterity and the greater scholarly good. I don't know if I want it or if I do not. STOP

Isn't the novel—that word that at other times means *new*—by now an old technology? We hear that thesis broadcast from the Teletype machines, the airwaves, the ever-expanding matrix of blogs, the glossy magazines. We've been hearing that for fifty years, and probably more. I don't think you can just declare a technology dead. On its own, it just hesitates, slows, and comes to a big dead STOP

A TELEX is a service still operated by Network Telex, a company based out of London (the UK ends up with many old technologies, maybe because of a more thorough respect for its technological forebears?), though you can't just send telegrams through them; they're not available directly to the consumer. Unlike faxes or photocopies, Telexes are considered to be legal documents—they are the only such technology that works in this way. Network Telex does have a service through which you can e-mail them a message, that then gets converted into TELEX and sent to the recipient of your choice. It is modulated, assuming several forms before it finds its recipient where it STOPs

I am on the train, coming back from Chicago late at night. A series of travel complications left me without a clear way home to Grand Rapids and my wife and cats, the shimmering idea of home, from Austin, Texas—at least without a way home by air. Thus the train, a Victorian technology. Here I hear many people (the travelers are mostly women, interestingly) speaking other languages, much more so than in the air. It is a gliding sort of nothingness to be cradled as we all are with the train's rhythm. The windows are dark, reflecting the inside of the train car, and there's an occasional light or break in the darkness, billboards lit up with messages for us, for me.

My laptop has wireless, of course—ingenious, so freeing, and I almost didn't get this technology installed, thinking it was almost useless—and I have spent most of the four hours of our ride caught between finishing Richard Powers's technological novel *Galatea 2.2* and watching occasional wireless bursts occur when our train slips through these signal nets cast out by hotspot networks of PCs with their base antennae or something else entirely. It comes in washes, like the radii of streetlights' illumination of the falling snow. It's intermittent, pulse-like. Just a glimpse of a connection to the bigger life around us, this newly whitened world (while I was in 85-degree weather walking the streets of Austin, it blizzarded back here and covered everything again in the usual winter shroud).

In these ways I have always loved methods of communication, the idea of complicated networks, of impossibly complex systems. I avidly check my e-mail, have spent years exploring the PBXes and trunks, the 2600 Hz blue box-tone access keys, and other pathways, illegalities, of the telephone system, all the dead ends and loopholes that appear in anything appropriately complex and convoluted. That telephone system, the big mess of Ma Bell and then the crush, the split-up monolith, the emergence of the baby Bells and AT&T's mama bear (SBC—formerly Southern Bell before they stripped the bell word out and reduced it to sleeker, more efficient initials—recently merged back into AT&T, which still stands for American Telephone and Telegraph, though they would not have you think of the telegraph: the name is just the name, a series of letters, a brand, like Kentucky Fried Chicken streamlined to KFC, the dread word *fried* excised). This, the glittering network of the telephone, my preferred method of pre-Internet communication, the technology that reduces our voices to then-analog, now-digital signals, strips away the edges of the frequencies of the human voice (which is why people sound different on the telephone), turns our voices into approximations of themselves. And the intermittent loveliness of Morse— a series of controlled bursts that, assembled, can be parsed back into language. Bitstreams, error correction, data packets, CRCs, compression algorithms. The elegance of code. I even find the idea of smoke signals, in their own way precursors to the telegraph, beautiful.

They are charms against aloneness. They are ways out of the labyrinth.

Perhaps that's why I'm drawn to text, to messages and missives, letters and letterettes, sentences that seem as though they will never end, and then they end. Even in my telephone days I used the telephone to transmit mostly data, not voice, communication. I hooked my machine into the big machine, which made its way to other machines. Books are hooks, are methods of communication, too, though slower. Speed is related perhaps to permanence. I remember playing a computer game on my old PC when I was younger. The machine had 256K of RAM and was PC-compatible (back when *compatible* didn't always mean exactly *compatible,* as in the old Tandy machines manufactured by RadioShack, which ran MS-DOS, but with weirdo quirks). The game was called *Starflight* and was billed as a space opera. It is still one of my all-time favorite games, though the decoder wheel that came with it (the game was published with a copy-protection decoder "security" wheel like so many others during the 1980s) was highly annoying. The plot of the game was convoluted, but two points bear discussion: the starships of this future world ran on a fuel called Endurium, and one of your goals was to survey and mine planets (always this return to the idea, the outline, of the mine) in order to collect Endurium, in order to power your ship to explore farther. The other plot arc was that the mythology of the game spoke of archetypal Ancients who had created much of the world and who had left the world behind and somehow mysteriously disappeared. The twist to the plot—I did beat the game, and it took me 200+ hours as I remember—was that you eventually realized that the Ancients *were* Endurium, that the fuel we used to power our spaceships was alive, but that the creatures (whatever they were) moved so slowly that a decade for us was like a second to them, so *we could not even observe their movements* and so thought them inanimate. It was a question of time frame. A huge revelation. The idea still gives me chills, and I am taken back there, in front of the glow of my amber monitor (we didn't have a color monitor; my friend Matt's RadioShack-brand Tandy had a sixteen-color monitor, though it didn't always run IBM software perfectly) as I realize this Game Truth, and my weird little world is forever changed.

There are web sites devoted to this game I played when I was ten. Many of them are now gone, though there are many links that still point to the space (if that is the word) where they once existed. Several promise links to dozens of other pages, and even though they made a sequel, *Starflight 2,* which I did own but did not beat (who knows why: maybe it bored me eventually, though through it I learned—and was proud to wield in class henceforth—the word *obsequious,* or maybe I had moved past that portion of my life). As late as 1997, there was talk of developing a *Starflight III,* a project that never took off, and you can still find online memorials to these games, the speculation around the

Starflight III left online after years of obsolescence (this game still has a lot of fans, it would appear—one web site I visited recorded 164,000+ hits since 1996, its last update). I have looked at these sites, and in my weaker moments spent hours poring over them, remembering, and remembering one of my own first searches for meaning, and in this way searching my past for meaning. This text is part reminiscence, part transmission to whatever will come after this or me or us, and part trying to figure out how to recapture what I had then: a fixity, a beautiful enveloping obsession. This track of thought is a hole, a drain that I could circle forever, a planet I could orbit slowly, like I do the mailbox some days, waiting for the U.S. Mail, this very old asynchronous technology, still delivered through all sorts of weather by hand (even sponsoring Lance Armstrong, more machine than man, one suspects) to at last arrive with some news from the glossy junk mail or real or other editorial world. I could ring and ring myself around the thing, considering it from the silent ice of space, a long-term obsession I can keep returning to, waiting for something to either fail or die, or failing that, from this distance, at least appear to move. STOP

APPENDIX: PARTS OF THE BOOK YOU MAY ADDITIONALLY ENJOY, SUCH AS AN APPENDIX

Although an appendix is not an essential part of every book, the possibilities and the uses of the device are many. Some kinds of material properly relegated to an appendix are explanations and elaborations not essential parts of the text but helpful to a reader seeking further clarification; texts of documents, laws, etc., illustrating the text; long lists, survey questionnaires, sometimes even charts or tables. The appendix should not be a repository for raw data that the author was unable to work into the text.

—The Chicago Manual of Style, 13th edition

It is hard for me, and thus for you, to avoid thinking about the artifact, the artifice, the artificialness of this thing you are holding. It is difficult for me to avoid thinking about the artifact I am writing, which consists of text in a small font that reaches from the left side of the page to the right and then spills down to the line below. I can't avoid talking about the thing of it, its—yes—form and beauty, the technology of the codex, the pages glued together in your hand with the perfect-bound spine and the provocative yet appropriate (we hope) cover art. Books have parts and are designed objects. They have form, both theoretical and physical, and you experience them as such. Because this is in its way a collection of essays, it seems reasonable to assume that you may flip around and start with any essay—this one included. I like the idea of reading the Appendix first, and if you are doing so, then you are in this way like me, and we can break bread together in fellowship. If not, if you have arrived here at the end of experiencing the artifact of the book with its enveloping whiteness, its pages turning and punctuating your reading experience, then I hope this will be a satisfying coda. It is not part of the book proper because it is not essential—or perhaps this is a lie.

I have doubtless lied several times, if not more, in this book. Most of these lies are unintentional and (I hope) harmless, and they come about through my own selective memory, or the editing process inherent in creating these things we call essays, which are in their own way quite formless (by accident and by design). Some of them are intentional: names have been changed to protect the etc. Because this is nonfiction, there is a greater attention to the factual goodness of the world, the verisimilitude that the prose has toward its subject: the world and all its mess and mash, its formlessness and occasional—surprising!—form. Some of the essays—in particular "Index for X and for the Origin of Fires," which takes its subject as the action of my novel-which-might-not-be-a-novel (oo!), *Other Electricities,* and which is more liberal in its invention and investigation than the other essays (perhaps this is obvious to you already, meaning that my technologies herein deployed—the words, the sentences, the syntax—have done their work) contain some confabulation. So: this is my method. Some run faster and looser with the idea of truth than journalistic nonfiction might feel comfortable with. I am not a journalist, and as such I am comfortable with it. I love comfort, the form of my body nestling perfectly into an enclosing form. Everything here is as true as I could make it; it all feels real and realized, and when I hold these essays—these lenses through which I have viewed the world—up to the world itself, they are the right fit.

I had breakfast in late 2005 at a local restaurant in Grand Rapids, Marie Catrib's, with an old friend. This was a particularly fraught meal for me because the central action of that book is based rather transparently on a murder that took place in my hometown when I was in middle school. The girl who was killed (it's almost always a girl, isn't it?) was my friend's sister. It was a terrible event for the whole community, and most obviously for my friend and for his family. I agonized more over the use of this plot arc in the book than I did anything else. While I applied a lot of fiction to this particular arc, I'd imagine that reading the book would be difficult for him and his family. He had just read the book and was coming through town. He had called the night before and wanted to meet and catch up. I chose Marie's because the woman who runs it used to run a restaurant (an earlier iteration of this one) in our hometown. She left for culinary school and opened up her new restaurant just a mile from my house. My wife and I eat there all the time, and it is a lovely place, incorporating folk art like I used to see in Alabama and photography by Joe Kirkish, a hometown photographer. It is a perfect crossroads for me, and when I eat there I often run into Houghton expatriates. So my friend and I ate and talked—a bit awkwardly, it's true; we hadn't seen each other in a few years—about his family, my book, my family, our collective health, his work, shared acquaintances, and truth.

Lunch went well, thank God. He liked the book, even if he seemed mystified, which is a fair response. Then again we are in the Midwest and we are men: we don't always say what (or all of what) we mean. That was fiction. That was strange, invented, tossed together. This is something else. Although in this book the characters from *Other Electricities* make appearances too. I'm not sure what to say about that.

I feel much more vulnerable here, in this book, on this page. Is that good or not? Can one become addicted to confession? Is it in itself worthy?

A friend of mine writes poems that are all completely true. Every character is my friend or someone she knows. There are no personas present. She wants to be in a way transparent. She is a vulnerability artist.

I am vulnerable and I am not.

It is a predicament.

I employ methods of obfuscation, of complication, of precipitation that stand between the word and world, between you and me.

Well, that's dramatic.

Not everything fits easily into the book. Much is left out. This book (in particular this appendix) is in its way a repository, a depository for a number of my secrets, almost all of which are true.

Perhaps it is strange to be remarking on the truth of one's own nonfiction, but I can assure you that some of the characters who are portrayed herein will take issue with some of the claims I have made about the world and their place in it. In this sense (again, this is nonfiction), I am operating without a safety net—that wide and helpful mesh, the sort provided by the sometime smokescreen of fiction. And given the recent (I write this in February 2006) flap over James Frey's invention in his own memoir (whatever that word means at this point in time),

I don't want to leave this stone facedown on the ground. James Frey's father teaches at the college where I am employed, Grand Valley State University, in Allendale, Michigan. Zip code: 49401. My office phone number is listed, and my office there (how odd to have an office at all, a dedicated space for official business) is located in Lake Ontario Hall, room 201. I tell you this so you have some facts to hold in front of you. I work on the second floor of this lovely new LEED (Leadership in Energy and Environmental Design: this is sexy green technology) building with lights that turn on and off according to carbon-dioxide emissions and patterns in the room, or so I'm told. It seems more likely, if less cool, that they are run by motion sensors. The design is such that it's much harder to waste energy, since the lights shut themselves off when no activity is detected. So when I sit at my desk that overlooks the ravines, the geologic gaps that split this campus and are beautiful and filled with trees and snow and space and light, the light turns off after about fifteen minutes. Unless I move toward the door, or someone opens up the door, or walks right by it outside. There's no way to turn it off or on myself except by motion in the area of the door. This feels like a metaphor, but for what I am not sure.

It is possible to hack the motion sensor, to modify its algorithm. I will not say definitively here whether this is something I have done or not.

My desk is largely cluttered—stacks and piles and heaps. Maybe it seems as though I am a busy person, or that I'm lazy. Either could be true. The thermostat (by the way you can use this as a verb, to control the temperature via a thermostat—though this time I mean the noun— and the adjective version is *thermostatic*, adverb: *thermostatically*) is set at its lowest setting, which is 55 degrees, because I like it cold. And I'm not sure it matters where I set it because the actual temperature does not seem to change; although I do get periodic complaints from frozen students who sit facing the ravine and asking me about fiction. You hear the occasional roar of forced air coming up through the vents into the offices from the basement, but I can't make sense of it. This is the problem with facts and phenomena: you can witness them but connecting them, placing them in proximity, in juxtaposition, cause and effect, is difficult. The air smells fresh and new. The world outside is not new, but it is beautiful and it creaks from side to side. It is winter, an easy winter thus far for Michigan, without lasting snow, and it will be spring in a matter of months. Still: these are facts. They are here and verifiable, at least until the world changes around them and leaves them without referent, floating all around us like ghosts, like abandoned technologies. Reading this page—my words—will get you somewhere else from where I am. These words, this book, these are indexes to another time, a past recorded experience set down here through this lens to you. It is like my card catalogue with headings but without cards. Every item is itself a mystery, a pointer to a ghostly space. But, for now, at this moment of conception, you can find me there (and you can always find me here, hanging around among these tenement, itinerant sentences: fixed, indexed, appendixed). You can find James Frey's dad here, too, somewhere on campus: and right now everyone in the literary world is talking about James Frey. I feel sorry for him, for them, for everybody, and probably some slaps are deserved. You can call up and ask his dad to clarify some of the facts recorded in the million-selling memoir book *A Million Little Pieces,* and I suspect he will decline to answer you. Don't bother him, though—it's rude, it's not his fault; he did not ask for this. In a way his son is an index (however bogus) to him and to their past lives together and apart. I'd ask you to do the same with my father, and I'm sure he would also think but decline to talk. This is what we do in the Midwest: we demur, we keep the hot side hot and the cool side cool, we keep the interiors of our lives from coming out. We hold our hands close to our bodies when it is so cold outside that we feel that our extremities just might freeze in spite of Thinsulate and layers of down and antiseptic insulating air. We are all about the surface tension, all exterior, outside the occasional mining expedition that connects the world with the inner, hotter world. We exist on the surface of the rock, and underneath is all the roiling magma. In warmer regions tensions might erupt.

In spite of this regional and cultural reticence, consider this a transmission.

What I am trying to tell you is this: in my own way, I love you. And you can trust me, mostly. I won't lead, wouldn't lead, haven't led you wrong. It would be bad form. But please know that if I do lead you wrong, I once thought it was right.

Please visit Ander Monson's web site
www.otherelectricities.com/neckdeep

NOTES

"Outline toward a Theory of the Mine Versus the Mind and the Harvard Outline": Thanks to the Harvard Archives for their help. Thanks to Sandy Huss for the lead on the bat information.

"I Have Been Thinking about Snow": The quotations from this piece are from the *OED*, unless otherwise noted. The form—like that used for the "Failure" essay—is after Chelsey Minnis's book *Zirconia*.

"Cranbrook Schools: Adventures in Bourgeois Topologies": Many thanks to Leonard Blackburn for his mathematical insight. Also, in its own way, thanks to Cranbrook Schools, a strange place. I am uncomfortable with the male gaze that shows up here, but am unsure what to make of it. On the whole I feel lucky to have survived, thus far, this life.

"Index for X and the Origin of Fires": This was the original index to my novel, *Other Electricities*, before it was trimmed out and became this something else. One hopes it still refers to a (or the) recognizable world. Some of the more factual entries are taken from the second edition of Paul L. Kirk's 1953 textbook, *Crime Investigation. Dead Kids 2* was an actual movie made by people I knew in college as a low-budget sequel to the original *Dead Kids*, a movie not worth tracking down, but filmed ostensibly at Knox College, where I went to school. And there's no way you'll be able to find the sequel, so you might as well not try. Several things were burned in the making of this essay.

"Fragments: On Dentistry": Thanks to Mark H., my student who wrote the essay about his dental hygienist that is referenced herein. Thanks to Heidi for the story about the camera. Thanks to Dr. W. for his good work—now mostly complete—in my mouth. Also for the nitrous. No thanks to Chick-fil-A: I curse your delicious sandwiches and your petrified fries.

"Subject to Wave Action: A There and a Back (with Orchestral Accompaniment)": As noted, the italicized quotes are from *H. M. S. Pinafore* by Gilbert and Sullivan. Thanks to the Lake Express LLC for some of the promotional material. And thanks to Victor for his friendship and appearance here.

"The Long Crush": Thanks to Innova and Discraft, makers of things good for long and curving flight, and to Leonard, and Eric O., Mike B., Eliot W., Mark E., Jeff H., Andy S., Matt V., Josh B., Victor S., Sean L., and the many others who have played slash will play along with me.

"Failure: A Meditation, Another Iteration (with Interruptions)": The unattributed stuff in italics is from "Weather's Effect on Failure," an article by Unified Engineering, Inc. <http://www.unified-eng.com/scitech/weather/weather.html>. I love my sources and my engineers, my father-in-law included. I have never actually visited Butte, Montana; I'm sure it's quite nice.

"After Form and Formlessness: Bodies, Boats, and Bathing": I also love my *Law & Order,* especially the *Criminal Intent* variation. This essay, like much of my work, is for my mother, circle within circles; form behind forms.

"The Big and Sometimes Colored Foam: Four Annotated Car Washes": I have probably thought too much about car washes. My Mazda Protegé is with me no longer, and I do not mourn it. My new car doesn't keep out the water completely either, as the tendril connecting the satellite radio to the antenna creates a small gap in the window sealing. There is still fear in my heart, though you will find my car recently washed.

"Afterword: Elegy for Telegram and *Starflight*": You can still send telegrams through Telegrams Canada <http://telegrams.ca> if you like. Since the demise of Western Union's service, Telegrams Canada has increased its service in this way. This negates the thesis of my essay, but it's still good news for telegrammers. Send me one, c/o GVSU, 326 LOH, One Campus Drive, Allendale, MI 49401. From their web site: "Telegrams are very different from air-letters! Telegrams Canada transmits your telegram by satellite or undersea cable to the destination country's telegraph office. It is then printed, placed in an envelope, and delivered by postman or special messenger. It's a fast, efficient, and very special way to send your thoughts and feelings thousands of miles away." I will be hoping for undersea cable, not the satellite. Thanks to Ali for her correspondence and her poetry. Thanks to my friend Matt F., one among many partners-in-crime for months of *Starflight*. No one was burned in the making of this essay.

"Appendix: Parts of the Book You May Additionally Enjoy, Such as an Appendix": "Keep the hot side hot and the cool side cool" refers to McDonald's McDLT, a semidelicious burger pretty much the same as their other burgers, but with the addition of ingenious and wasteful split packaging. I think of the Joy Division song "Transmission" in the last paragraphs. You should, too.

"Notes": Thanks especially to Alicia Holmes for suggesting that "Index for X . . ." is in fact nonfiction. Unless I am sued, in which case I reserve the right to retract my thanks. To John D'Agata for publishing a couple of these, for being interesting and interested, and for selecting "Index for X . . ." for the Annie Dillard Award in Creative Nonfiction from the *Bellingham Review*. To Michael Martone and Sandy Huss. To Sophia Kartsonis, who looked at this manuscript and helped to make it less crappy. To Matt McGowan for his belief and sure hand at the helm finding this beast a home. To Robert Polito, who chose this out of the ether for the Nonfiction Prize. To Katie, Fiona, and Anne for their belief and for saving me from some of my own worst writerly tendencies. To Mary, Janna, and everyone at Graywolf for having their way with it, allowing me to have my way with it, for holding it close to their collective heart, and for indulging my decoder fixations (I hope you, dear reader, got one). Thanks to the editors who published sections of this book in their great magazines. Thanks to my colleagues at Grand Valley State University, the administration, and my students for their support. And to the writers I like the best, my friends, my comrades-in-arms, with an extra side of love. To the wide sky of my family and the absolute support of my wife. To Alabama, Iowa, Illinois, Saudi Arabia, and Michigan. And to the lakes, my lakes, which I remain suspended in.

THE GRAYWOLF PRESS NONFICTION PRIZE

Neck Deep and Other Predicaments by Ander Monson is the 2006 winner of the Graywolf Press Nonfiction Prize. Graywolf awards this prize annually to a previously unpublished, full-length work of outstanding literary nonfiction by a writer who is not yet established in the genre. The 2005 winner was *Frantic Transmissions to and from Los Angeles: An Accidental Memoir* by Kate Braverman.

The Graywolf Press Nonfiction Prize seeks to acknowledge—and honor— the great traditions of literary nonfiction, extending from Robert Burton and Thomas Browne in the seventeenth century through Daniel Defoe and Lytton Strachey and on to James Baldwin, Joan Didion, and Jamaica Kincaid in our own time. Whether grounded in observation, autobiography, or research, much of the most beautiful, daring, and original writing over the past few decades can be categorized as nonfiction. Graywolf is excited to increase its commitment to this evolving and dynamic genre.

The prize is judged by Robert Polito, author of *Savage Art: A Biography of Jim Thompson, Doubles,* and *A Reader's Guide to James Merrill's The Changing Light at Sandover,* and Director of the Graduate Writing Program at the New School in New York City.

The Graywolf Press Nonfiction Prize is funded in part by endowed gifts from the Arsham Ohanessian Charitable Remainder Unitrust and the Ruth Easton Trust of the Edelstein Family Foundation.

Arsham Ohanessian, an Armenian born in Iraq who came to the United States in 1952, was an avid reader and a tireless advocate for human rights and peace. He strongly believed in the power of literature and education to make a positive impact on humanity.

Ruth Easton, born in North Branch, Minnesota, was a Broadway actress in the 1920s and 1930s. The Ruth Easton Trust of the Edelstein Family Foundation is pleased to support the work of emerging artists and writers in her honor.

Graywolf Press is grateful to Arsham Ohanessian and Ruth Easton for their generous support.

ANDER MONSON lives in Michigan, where he edits the magazine *DIAGRAM* and the New Michigan Press. He is the author of two other books: a novel, *Other Electricities* (Sarabande Books, 2005) and a poetry collection, *Vacationland* (Tupelo Press, 2005). He teaches at Grand Valley State University. His web site is: www.otherelectricities.com

Neck Deep and Other Predicaments has been typeset in Minion Pro, a typeface designed by Robert Slimbach and issued by Adobe in 1989. Book design by Wendy Holdman. Composition at Prism Publishing Center. Manufactured by Friesens on acid-free paper.